Congregationalism
A Restaten

by

DANIEL JENKINS

HARPER AND BROTHERS
New York

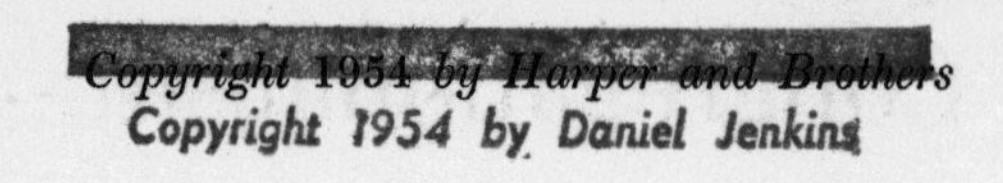

Printed in Great Britain

Contents

Foreword

Part of the material in this book has been presented, in different forms, to some of my students at the University of Chicago and to my congregation at Oxted. I am grateful to both groups for their interest and encouragement. I am particularly grateful to a fellow member of the Oxted church, who corrected the proofs and prepared the Index. My colleague at the University of Chicago, Professor Daniel Day Williams, and the Secretary of the Congregational Union of England and Wales, Dr. L. E. Cooke, both very kindly read the book and made valuable suggestions.

D.J.

I

Congregationalism and the Ecumenical Movement

'The ecumenical movement', said Archbishop Temple in a much-quoted phrase, 'is the great new fact of our era.' It is a phrase, however, which derives its effect as much from the amount of surprise it evokes as from the amount of obvious truth which it contains. For the number of people who could honestly make such a claim for the ecumenical movement is not large. There are not a few, even among church members, who have not so much as heard that there is an ecumenical movement and of those who have, many of them think of it as something almost as esoteric as its name, an activity of prominent ecclesiastics who meet together at surprisingly frequent intervals in one or other of the pleasanter large cities of the world for elaborate and highly technical conferences. The more percipient among ordinary church members may suspect a connection between this activity and the marked improvement in relations between the churches in their immediate neighbourhood but, for the most part, they find it hard to see how it is likely radically to affect their way of understanding the Christian faith and leading the Christian life.

Yet, although it was one of Archbishop Temple's engaging characteristics that he was sometimes not averse to throwing episcopal caution to the winds in pursuit of an exciting new idea, he was evidently fully aware of the implications of his statement in making it when he did. It was not made in the heat of the moment at a public meeting convened by enthusiasts to promote their cause. It was spoken at his enthronement as Archbishop of Canterbury in the early days of the Second World War, as part of one of the most solemn and carefully worded utterances of his life. What is more, it was backed up by an almost lifelong dedication to the ecumenical cause.

What was true of Archbishop Temple is no less true of many other leading churchmen today. Despite cynical opinions to the contrary, highly placed ecclesiastical officers are among the busiest and most hard pressed of men and a rash eagerness to embrace the latest new craze which comes along is not one of their characteristic weaknesses. If a large number of the outstanding leaders of the churches today, leaders in spiritual and intellectual achievements as well as holders of official positions, give a substantial part of their time to the service of the ecumenical movement, the likelihood is that it is others rather than they who are misled as to its importance. If they see it to be 'the great new fact of our era', the rest of us would do well to consider whether we have understood it aright and whether we have fully grasped all its implications for our own church and the way we try to live the Christian life.

One frequent source of misunderstanding is the fact that the nature of the ecumenical movement can very easily be misrepresented. It is not merely an agency for holding international conferences of Christians, who come together to draw inspiration from each others' company, register the present state of their agreements and differences and attempt some cautious progress, and who then offer messages to the world which are so carefully drafted that it sometimes requires both theological and diplomatic training to interpret them. Nor is it solely a movement for the promotion of reunion and for expressing Christian fellowship among the churches of different nations through mutual aid, although these activities are of central importance in its life. Nor yet is it to be exclusively identified with the World Council of Churches and the various national and regional councils which are its primary organizational expressions. It can, perhaps, be most generally described as a movement for the renewal and re-integration of the divided parts of Christ's Church on earth, in the light of a fresh vision of the Church as a single reality given by Christ as part of His Gospel.

It is not the purpose of this book to elaborate upon what is involved in this definition of the ecumenical movement but this much should be noted because it throws light on the kind of re-interpretation of itself which participation in the movement demands of Congregationalism. What brings us together in ecumenical activity is not enthusiasm for organizational unity but a fresh understanding, given in our encounter with each other, of what the New Testament means by the Church of Jesus Christ. The ecumenical vision is, above all else, a renewed vision of Christ and of the way Christ is related to all His people, of every denomination and country and period in history. It enables members of a particular church to see other churches as they are 'in Christ' and to see Christ manifest in the other churches.[1] It carries with it a compulsion to draw nearer to other churches 'in Christ' because it teaches us that we cannot properly follow Christ Himself without doing so. The compulsion remains even if the differences between other churches and one's own may seem, for the present, to be insuperable. To be disillusioned with the ecumenical movement, as people sometimes are, because it does not rapidly and painlessly achieve widespread organizational reunion is to display a misapprehension of the distinctively ecumenical vision. For what that vision reveals is a unity lying behind all

[1] For a very helpful statement of this idea see *Vision and Action: the Problem of Ecumenism*, by L. A. Zander (Gollancz, London, 1952), pp. 205–10.

the differences between the churches which it is the duty of those who see it to bring out and express in the midst of the contradictions and confusions of authority and liturgy and teaching and organization which arise both because of the sinfulness of men and because of the incalculable movement of the Spirit amidst the changes of history. The reunion of this particular denomination with that may or may not be an immediate practical possibility. The external unity of all believers in one organization may never reach perfect and final expression on this earth. But the compulsion remains upon all who have seen this vision to be ministers of Christ's reconciling grace among the churches and to bring them to that unity of heart and mind and wholeness of purpose which is His will for all His people.

It is because they have for so long neglected this side of their duty that this has come home with peculiar force to churches in considering their relations with other churches, but it is no less important to realize that it has far-reaching consequences for each church's understanding of itself. This is an aspect of the ecumenical movement which has not yet been sufficiently emphasized, a fact which may account for some of the frustration which is experienced in relation to the movement in various quarters today. Yet it is clearly unreal to suppose that a church can enter into deep communion in Christ with another church without itself undergoing a painful inner transformation. There is an internal as well as an external side to a church's participation in the ecumenical movement and it is, in many ways, the more important.

It is an experience so common as almost to be universal in ecumenical encounters that, after the initial shock of discovering that members of other churches have also experienced the same unifying vision of Christ's purpose for His whole Church, the representatives of a particular church should then turn round to each other and say, 'But where, in the light of all this that has happened to us, do we as a denomination now stand?' They are compelled to ask themselves what it is that has justified them in remaining separate for so long from those who are so clearly their brethren and what they have usefully to contribute to the conversation which has been re-opened. This occurs in its most striking form among those Protestant bodies which may have had little occasion to think much about these matters in the past. Thus it is well known that it is participation in the ecumenical movement which has prompted the Methodist Church in England to review and set out in systematic form, practically for the first time, what its own teaching is about the nature of the Church. But, although their history and character have made them more familiar with these questions and although they are constitutionally less ready to admit inadequacies in their own tradition, the effect on the inner life of churches of more Catholic type has been hardly less serious.

This revived denominational self-consciousness is, in itself, inevitable and healthy. It is a sign that the ecumenical movement has really 'taken', that it has worked itself inside a church's own system, and it is a necessary condition which must be present before a genuine change of attitude can take place. But, as experience is beginning to show, it can also be very dangerous if its full challenge is not met and a church shrinks from going on to take the next step, which is to look at itself, not only defensively in relation to other churches, but also positively as a church of which God may be requiring some new departure, in the light of the deeper insight into its own place in the fulfilment of His purpose which participation in the ecumenical movement has brought it. Only if it does that can the movement justify the claim to be 'the great new fact of our era' in terms of the life of a particular church.

All organizations are exposed to the sin of self-righteousness, and the stronger the grip they have upon their adherents the greater the danger. This has often enough been pointed out in the case of states or nations, which will perpetrate deeds in their corporate capacity which most of their individual members would never dream of committing to further their personal interest. It is not always so clearly seen, especially by churchmen, that churches, also, receive no exemption from the same temptation. Protestants constantly complain against those churches which call themselves Catholic, and especially the Roman Catholic Church, that so far from being conscious of the dangers of this corporate self-righteousness and trying to safeguard themselves against it, they make a virtue of it and so organize themselves as to buttress and justify it. But Protestants also need to remember that they have no ground for supposing that they have any automatic freedom from this danger. It is too deep-rooted in the nature of society for that to be likely. What is more, there is enough experience from the conduct of international affairs since the war to remind us that for people to meet does not of itself necessarily produce either agreement or understanding. While the worst meeting is probably always at least one degree better than open warfare, a meeting can also produce more passionate defensiveness and self-righteousness than would have arisen if no confrontation had taken place.

It is the belief, grounded in experience, of those who lead the ecumenical movement that the movement is sufficiently blessed by the Holy Spirit to enable churches to resist this temptation but they will do so only if they frankly recognize it as a temptation and take steps to overcome it. It is obviously particularly acute precisely at the point where a church is challenged to make a radically new departure which causes it to venture into the unknown and to cast aside vested interests and cherished preconceptions. Besides, as Dr. H. P. Van Dusen has observed, churches have begun to develop a habit of allowing the pioneering work in many new directions to be done by interdenominational bodies and, once its character has been established, of moving in and building parallel organization to do the same work, on a purely denominational basis.[1] This has happened with missionary societies and with work among students and there are numerous signs, with the recent rapid extension of 'Ecumenical Methodism' and the 'Lutheran World Federation' and similar bodies, that the same could happen in regard to the ecumenical movement. Only a renewal of the true ecumenical vision and a determined effort to restate its own distinctive vocation in its light can save a church, especially if it is a strong and numerous one, from moving in this direction.

The following pages offer a modest attempt at such a restatement on behalf of one particular denomination. They will try to look at Congregationalism in the setting of the ecumenical movement, in order both to discover what light the ecumenical vision and the experience of other churches throws on Congregationalism's understanding of itself and to interpret it to other churches. What 'internal ecumenicity' means can only be discovered by each person in terms of the life of that church in which he lives and of which he is a responsible member. This essay will, however, fail of its purpose if it does not stimulate members of other churches to undertake similar essays on behalf of their own denominations. The next step forward in the conversation between the churches over matters of faith and order may be, not the continued reaffirmation of the distinctive positions of the churches over against each other, but the re-interpretation of each church's particular vocation in the setting of the whole.

What is meant by this should become clearer in detail as our argument proceeds, but it may be useful to bear in mind these general considerations before we embark upon it. First, to consider one's own church in the setting of the whole does

[1] See his article, 'Councils in Crisis' in *Theology Today*, January 1953.

not merely mean considering it in relation to what other churches are doing, although that is, of course, an important part of it. It also means looking at it anew in the light of a fresh understanding of the New Testament conception of the Church. All churches like to claim that they are more faithful to that conception than any others but it is precisely such efforts at self-justification which this fresh understanding calls into question. The New Testament does not present us with a model Church whose external characteristics we should strive to copy in every detail nor even with an ideal Church to which we should aspire. It confronts us with the presence of the living Christ in the Spirit, who reconciles men to God and through that reconciliation gives them a new relationship of unity and peace with each other and guides them through their lives. The understanding of the Church in the New Testament which has arisen in the ecumenical movement[1] challenges all the attempts of the denominations to trim that conception to suit their own domestic convenience and forces them to listen to the voice of Christ concerning His Church in a new and more radical way. It becomes a call to repentance, not merely for having failed to live up to a church's own ideal of itself but also for having possessed an inadequate and misleading ideal. This is the risk which each church must run in looking at itself in the setting of the whole. Its basis is called again into question by the One who has the right to do so, Christ who is Himself the wholeness of the Church and who ever and anew reasserts His lordship over the churches.

Secondly, in the light of this renewed vision of the divine purpose for the Church and of the consequent realization of its own failures, each church must humbly seek from other

[1] See the essays, 'The Universal Church in God's Design', prepared for the Amsterdam Conference of 1948 and published as the first part of *Man's Disorder and God's Design* (S.C.M., London, and Harpers, New York).

churches ways of making up that which is lacking in its own life and of working with them more adequately to realize the divine purpose. This, once more, is far removed from the common attitude of seeking to justify the claims of one's own church in the face of the counter-claims of other churches. It means, as we have seen, trying to look at others as they are 'in Christ', with the recognition that He has dealings with them as He has with us. Like us, they have their failures and need our help as we need theirs, yet they will have seen some aspects of His will denied to us and they hold in trust treasures of grace which we would do well to covet. Few actions are more rewarding than to look at other churches in this positive and expectant way and then to turn back and look at ourselves with what we have seen fresh in our minds. It leads not only to a revaluation of others but also sometimes to startling discoveries about ourselves. Thus a later chapter will try to prove that ecumenical experience demonstrates that the Congregational witness on behalf of spiritual freedom is much less striking and original than many of our spokesmen have been prepared to admit but that our emphasis on the responsible participation of ordinary church members in reaching ecclesiastical decisions and our conception of the function of a deacon are even more valuable contributions to the life of the Great Church than had been supposed.

Thirdly, this procedure implies that a church will make a determined effort to look at itself not only in terms of the doctrines it professes nor even as a religious movement in the narrow sense but as a cultural phenomenon. The word 'culture' here, of course, is used not simply to refer to the arts but in the most general sense to describe a church's whole way of looking at things, manner of life, influence and atmosphere. It means that a church should try to look at itself 'in the round', as an institution set not only in the midst of other churches but in the midst of society in general and affecting the ordinary life of the world at many points. The connection of this with the ecumenical movement is closer than might first appear. The other side of the re-integration of the divided parts of the life of the Church is the re-integration of the divided parts of the common life of mankind. The sphere of Christian obedience is not that small part of life which is arbitrarily defined as 'religious' or 'ecclesiastical'. All parts of human existence are brought under the dominion of Christ. Churches exist in the midst of the ordinary, everyday, 'secular' life of men and even the most narrowly defined of them are involved with that life in innumerable ways. A re-integration of the Church which has no renewing and reconciling effect on the society around it is unreal and, indeed, corrupt. For it is bound to mean that a large part of the lives even of those who make up the membership of the church is unaffected by it. This has been clearly recognized by those who lead the ecumenical movement almost from the outset, because they have seen questions of 'Life and Work' to be their proper domain just as much as those of 'Faith and Order' and have deliberately fused the two interests in the work of the World Council of Churches.

At the same time, it is doubtful whether, even in the ecumenical movement, all the implications of this fact have been grasped, especially as they apply to the study of churches themselves. Much attention has been paid recently to the non-theological factors which divide churches and the point has been made that they often have as much influence in determining the relations of churches to each other as matters of doctrine and order. That is true, but so far it has prompted very little study of churches from the cultural point of view. This is the more regrettable because the resources of the modern social sciences are now available and can greatly aid us in this study. It is true that to look at churches from the sociological point of view or in terms of their relations to economic forces or the general artistic or intellectual influence of their age does not exhaust their meaning and that it is the occupational temptation of those who think in these terms to assume that it does. But there is no reason why churchmen should refuse the help which can come from these quarters, especially as they of all people should be well equipped to resist the temptation of excessive specialism which it might bring. The Church is the domain of the Holy Spirit and it is, finally, in terms of what the Holy Spirit is saying to and through our churches that we must interpret their significance. But to invoke the Holy Spirit is not a mere refuge for ignorance. To look at our churches as cultural phenomena may very well enable us to see more clearly where the Holy Spirit has been acting and where we have been resisting the Spirit, for, once more, the Spirit does not meet men only within the narrowly ecclesiastical realm but along the whole range of their lives. This book will, therefore, deal not only with the worship and teaching of Congregationalism, but also with such matters as its social and political influence, its effect on the arts and on politics, the kind of common life it produces among its members, and the reasons for its evangelistic successes and failures.

There is one other consideration which needs to be mentioned in explaining the purpose of this book. It is of a different character from those already dealt with. Congregationalism has, in the last fifty years, passed through a period of confusion about its own vocation and even about its relation to the historic Gospel. It was not unique among churches in this respect and if it suffered to a greater degree than some others it may have been partly because it faced so courageously the implications of the new knowledge brought by Biblical Criticism and the readjustment of outlook caused by modern science. Its casualties in this enterprise have not been light and over the last generation many Congregational churches have shown a marked weakening both in religious and intellectual quality. Today, however, much of the confusion has passed and many of the leaders of Congregationalism speak with more insight and conviction about the Gospel and the Church than was customary, say, a quarter of a century ago. The programme of the Saint Andrews International Congregational Council of 1953 is clear proof of this. The ecumenical movement itself cannot claim all the credit for this change. The theological revival associated with the name of Barth, which has prompted fresh interest in the work of our own P. T. Forsyth, the new emphasis on Biblical Theology, of which Congregational scholars have been among the chief exponents and the re-interpretation of the work of the Independent divines of the seventeenth century, have all played their part. But much of this work has been stimulated by ecumenical contacts and the re-definition of Congregational churchmanship which is taking place today is directly due to the influence of other churches. Since most theological work today is carried on in terms of the ecumenical discussion, ecumenical thinking is likely to have an increasingly large part to play in determining the future development of Congregationalism.

The danger inherent in this situation is that the new attitude of the leaders of Congregationalism may not find its response quickly enough among the rank and file of members and even of ministers of Congregational churches. It was pointed out at the beginning that many faithful members of churches have not so much as heard that there is an ecumenical movement and that even among those who have there is widespread misunderstanding of its nature. It is important, therefore, that some of its implications for Congregationalism should be clearly brought out and expressed in concrete terms. Otherwise, what should be a movement of revival will serve only to make confusion worse confounded. The likelihood of this happening is all the greater because many of the most ecumenically minded leaders of Congregationalism are in teaching or administrative posts which do not always bring them into intimate contacts with ordinary members of churches.

It would be naïve indeed for the writer to imagine that he was in a good position to interpret the ecumenical movement to Congregationalism in general or to claim that he could speak with any authority as an interpreter of 'the mind of Congregationalism' to other churches. He is fully aware of the extent to which his view of Congregationalism is conditioned by his own particular experience, which is not typical of Congregationalists. But perhaps his unusual position as a minister of an English Congregational church who has frequent opportunities of studying Congregationalism in the U.S.A. and who also possesses a fairly extensive acquaintance with various aspects of the ecumenical movement may serve not only to make it easier for him to explain Congregationalism to other churches but also to help his fellow-Congregationalists look at themselves in a different light and take account of factors in their situation which are commonly neglected or ignored.

II

What is Congregationalism Like?

One of the greatest problems confronting those who would bring the churches closer together is the fact that churches have only the vaguest ideas of what churches other than their own are like. Theologians may by now be familiar with the teachings of the various churches and may enjoy personal acquaintance and even friendship with those of other communions but they share a common professional interest and academic background. Yet even their notions of what the ordinary members of other churches are like are often both over-simple and out of date and what is true of theologians is likely to be even more true of the attitude of ordinary members themselves, especially when strong inherited attitudes of suspicion and snobbery enter in, as they only too frequently do. This is particularly the case in England, where it is still possible to meet devout and influential Anglicans who are conditioned in their thinking about reunion by a hazy belief that all Nonconformists are grocers and Nonconformists who assume that communion with the Church of England will mean having to touch their forelocks to the squire and general conformity with the social patterns of Victorian village life. No real progress in understanding can be made unless such careless and childish ideas are abandoned and accurate and up-to-date knowledge substituted. Before we go on to consider what the prospects for Congregationalism are in the light of the ecumenical movement, therefore, it may be as well that our memories should be refreshed as to the history and present character of the denomination. This may possibly be of some service to Congregationalists themselves, as well as to members of other churches.

Congregational churches as separate bodies arose out of the Reformation in England. Their founders were on the left wing of the Puritan party in the Church of England in Elizabethan times. Like the Presbyterians, to whom they were closely related, they sought a reformation of the English Church more radical than that proposed by the Queen and her advisers but, unlike most of the Presbyterians, they were not confident of being able to persuade the authorities to agree to such a reformation. Their watchword was 'Reformation without tarying for anie' and they started to set up independent congregations. This led them into trouble and, under the leadership of the turbulent Robert Browne, some of them emigrated to Holland and set up churches there, but remained in contact with the growing congregations in England. These were persecuted and three prominent leaders, Henry Barrow, John Greenwood and John Penry, were martyred for their faith. Persecution led many others to flee to Holland and it was from there that the first New England emigrants set out. Separatism continued to grow in England, however, and Laud's policy united many non-Separatist Puritans with the Separatists, prompting some of them to throw in their lot with the New England settlers. With the rise of the dispute between Parliament and the King, the strength of Puritanism rapidly grew. The Long Parliament appointed the Westminster Assembly of Divines to advise it concerning a further reformation of the Church. The majority of the Assembly were Presbyterians, under strong Scottish influence, and they proposed that England adopt the Solemn League and Covenant and a Presbyterian established church. This did not win widespread support, however, and the voices of the Independent minority, who were in sympathy with the doctrinal statements in the Westminster Confession but who disagreed over the rights of each congregation to order its own affairs and over liberty of conscience, became increasingly powerful. With the rise of Cromwell and the Army, Presbyterianism was defeated, and during the Protectorate the Independents were the strongest single religious influence. Their own representatives were placed in positions of leadership, although there was widespread toleration, extending in some cases to Episcopalians. This was a period of rich theological development, in which the principles of Independency were defined and justified by men of deep learning and catholic vision, notably John Owen and Thomas Goodwin. With the Restoration, however, all was changed, and the Act of Uniformity was quickly passed. On Saint Bartholomew's Day 1662, two thousand ministers left their livings in the Church of England and modern Dissent was born.

The majority of two thousand ejected ministers were Presbyterians rather than Independents. The circumstances of the ensuing persecution, however, encouraged the organization of churches on the Independent model, as it was difficult to maintain the close and centralized Presbyterian order, and Baptist and Independent or, as they began now to be called, Congregationalist churches tended to grow at the expense of the Presbyterians. The Revolution of 1688 and the Toleration Act made life more possible for Dissenters and their cause flourished. They suffered a temporary setback under Queen Anne but her death in 1714 and the accession of the House of Hanover prevented the realization of their worst fears. The limited prosperity which they enjoyed in the earlier part of the eighteenth century did not, however, produce spectacular spiritual results among Congregationalists. It is true that most of them resisted the drift to Arianism which overtook Presbyterianism, that there were outstanding ministries of differing kinds like those of Isaac Watts and

Philip Doddridge, and that the Dissenting Academies made a striking contribution to national education. But there was a strong decline in church sense among them and they seemed content with their mediocre lot.

The Evangelical Revival was, however, a quickening influence in Congregationalism as in other churches, prompting them to a new evangelistic zeal which found expression in the founding in 1795 of the London Missionary Society, one of the first of the modern missionary societies. Dissenters were to be found more among the trading and manufacturing classes than among the landed gentry and the Industrial Revolution greatly increased their numbers and influence. Throughout the nineteenth century, therefore, their record is one of persistent expansion and many of the barriers which had cut them off from the main stream of the nation's life were broken down. This movement reached its climax in the Liberal victory in the election of 1906, which gave Nonconformity, and especially Congregationalism, an influence in the councils of the country which it had not had since Cromwell's day. But the war of 1914 soon descended and great new forces were let loose in the life of the world to which Congregationalism, like most other churches, has not yet fully adjusted itself.

The influential part that Congregationalism has played in the development of America is not always realized. It is not always clearly grasped even that the Pilgrim Fathers were Congregationalists. It is true that many of the original settlers in New England came from non-Separatist Puritanism in England and that the dominant influence in the Massachusetts Bay Colony in particular was in spirit more akin to Presbyterianism than to Independency but the organization was Congregational and its Congregational character became more and more pronounced as time went on. In contrast to the situation in England, Congregationalism became the established church in Massachusetts and Connecticut and remained so until well on into the nineteenth century. It produced many great theologians, notable among them Jonathan Edwards, and was directly instrumental in founding many of the most famous of the older American educational institutions such as Harvard and Yale. Towards the end of the eighteenth century and in the early nineteenth century, it was affected by the rise of Unitarianism, especially in the Boston area, which estranged many of the leading American families from Congregationalism and which greatly weakened the Congregational connection with Harvard, but Congregationalism remained the dominant church in New England until the twentieth century and is still firmly entrenched there. It made and continues to make little impression on the South and, through a compact with the Presbyterians which was made in the early nineteenth century, it has few churches in the Middle Atlantic states, but after the opening of the rich farmlands of the Middle West, New England Yankees were in the forefront of the settlers. They took their Congregational churches and colleges and democratic politics with them and a large part of the professional and academic population of the Middle West is Congregationalist to this day. They were not so successful, however, in evangelizing the later frontier communities and in appealing to the large masses of simple people who grew up in them and the initiative passed to the Methodist and various kinds of Baptist churches, who were followed later by churches of continental European origin.

Two things stand out very clearly from the history of Congregationalism. The first is that, despite their considerable influence upon the life of England and Wales and the U.S.A., Congregational churches make up one of the smaller groups among the churches of the world. In numbers they are a mite compared to the great Roman Catholic, Orthodox, Lutheran, and Presbyterian Reformed churches and little more than a pygmy by the side of such bodies as the Anglican, the

Methodist, and the Baptist. There are probably not many more than about two million members of Congregational churches in the world, although the number in closely related churches is considerably larger and it is worth remembering that membership statistics stand for a good deal more in Congregational churches than they do in, say, Roman Catholic or European Lutheran churches.

Secondly, apart from the Welsh-speaking churches of Wales, and some of the Younger Churches formed through the work of missionaries, Congregational churches are found almost exclusively in English-speaking countries. In England itself, they are a well established, medium-sized denomination, considerably smaller than the Church of England and barely half the size of the Methodists, but similar in size to the Baptists and considerably larger than the English Presbyterians, Unitarians, and the Society of Friends. In Wales they are fairly strong, in Scotland fairly weak, except in the large cities, and in Ireland they maintain only a vestigial existence. Although they have been so influential in the history of the United States, even there they are not a very numerous body, proportionately only slightly stronger than in England. In 1932 they united with a smaller body, found chiefly in the Upper South, the Christians, and the denomination in the U.S.A. is now known as the Congregational-Christian body. Their General Council recently voted in favour of a merger with the Evangelical and Reformed Church of the U.S.A., a church of German Presbyterian and Lutheran origin which claims Reinhold Niebuhr and Paul Tillich among its members, but the completion of the merger is held up by a lawsuit contesting its validity which a Congregationalist minority has seen fit to undertake.

Within the British Commonwealth the progress of Congregationalism has not been spectacular. The fairly strong Congregational church in Canada united in the 1920's with the

Methodists and many Presbyterians to form the powerful United Church of Canada. But in South Africa their strength is only moderate, with a numerical preponderance among the coloured population. And in New Zealand and Australia they are notably weak, having lost ground alarmingly in Australia in the last thirty years, where other churches of similar type have been making progress.[1]

There are some churches on the continent of Europe which are Congregational in form and are in association with the International Congregational Council. Chief among them are the Remonstrant Church in Holland and the Swedish Mission Covenant Church. There are, however, undoubted differences in doctrine and in spirit between them and the Congregational churches of the English-speaking world and their relationships with them remain somewhat tentative.

What kind of people are Congregationalists? Once again, a striking homogeneity emerges. Thomas Binney, a well-known London minister of the nineteenth century, described the Congregationalists of his day as people 'of the middling sort', and the description remains very apt. In England, their churches are those of the middle classes of the towns and cities. Rural Congregationalism, never very strong, is now extremely weak. This is one reason why the denomination's strength is frequently underestimated by many Southern Englishmen, who tend to maintain the fiction that all English people live either in the country or in the West End of London. It is not surprising, therefore, that the number of the old-established nobility and gentry of England who are Congregationalists should be very small indeed. On the other hand, Congregationalism's hold upon the working-classes has never been very strong. The rough rule appears to be that the

[1] See an article by Principal E. S. Kiek on 'The Religious Situation in Australia', in the *Congregational Quarterly* for January 1952, vol. xxx, No. 1.

more skilled the workman the more likely is he to be a Congregationalist and the larger the town the less effective the influence of Congregationalism upon its working-class population. The only exceptions to this are found in Wales, where rural Congregationalism is also strong, and in some of the smaller milling communities of Yorkshire and Lancashire, together with a few places in the Midlands and West Country where Dissenters founded academies or mills or factories in old market towns several generations ago.[1] But the main strength of English Congregationalism is undoubtedly to be found in the comfortable residential districts of the great cities and large towns.

Society is less stratified now than it was when Charles Booth made his survey of *Life and Labour of the People in London* over fifty years ago but the pattern of church life which he discovered remains strikingly applicable in the changed circumstances of today. In the West End and its fashionable adjuncts, Kensington, Chelsea, and Bayswater, Congregationalism had only a few churches while Anglicanism reigned supreme. In the East End, Congregationalism's influence was exerted chiefly through missions. In the ordinary humble, respectable suburbs it was much stronger but not as strong as Methodism and the Baptists. But in the prosperous and successful suburbs of those late Victorian days, Hampstead, Clapham, Brixton, Highbury, it reached its zenith. The population has, of course, shifted greatly since Booth's day. Old suburbs have 'gone down' and people have moved much further out but there has been surprisingly little change in the relation of Congregational churches to the general community. Thus today, the man who lives in his own house in Mill Hill or Winchmore Hill or Bromley or Purley

[1] Incidentally some of the most agreeable and firmly based Congregational churches are to be found in these towns. Trowbridge, Newport Pagnell, and Basingstoke are cases in point.

or, for that matter, in Hale or Sutton Coldfield or Redland Park, or who has retired from any of those places to Bournemouth or Westcliff or St. Anne's, the man who owns a large shop or a small factory, who is an accountant or a bank manager, or a secondary school master or a senior official in local government, is as likely to be a Congregationalist as anything else. And unless he happens to live in Wales or a few exceptional places of the kind which have been mentioned, if he is another type of person living in another type of neighbourhood, the chances that he will be a Congregationalist are very much smaller. Congregational churches are at their strongest, apart from a diminishing number of central churches like Carrs Lane, Birmingham, in districts of cities where the density of population is lightest and at their weakest where it is heaviest.

The situation is not dissimilar in the United States, though with differences which reflect the differing history of that country. Broadly speaking, the people in American Congregational churches are obviously the first cousins of those found in England but their circumstances have encouraged their greater prosperity and influence. As we have seen, Congregational churches used to be the established churches in New England and that fact is inevitably reflected in their present condition. They share with the Unitarians many of the oldest and most beautiful buildings and are more often the main churches of the community, although their position in this respect is modified by the depopulation of the New England countryside and the great influx of immigrants, often Catholics, into the towns. They tend to have more social leaders in their ranks than their English opposite numbers but have, if anything, even fewer ordinary working people. Yet there will be a very similar form of worship and a similar democratic, responsible spirit among the members of the congregation. And what is true of New England will be even more true, if possible, of the Middle West and the Far West. In these days, indeed, the most typical and flourishing of all Congregational churches are to be found in this region, chiefly in the suburbs of large cities, with ever-growing outposts in the less eccentric parts of Southern California, to which the members of mid-Western churches retire in large numbers.

Congregationalism, therefore, is not only restricted to English-speaking and related countries but also very largely to people of a particular type who live in particular neighbourhoods within these countries. The significance of this will have to be pondered upon later.

In faith and order, Congregationalism holds something of the 'middling' position in Protestantism that its members have in their own societies, although in the setting of the whole of Christendom, including Rome and the Orthodox East, they will appear to be well to the left. Every church likes to think of itself as a 'bridge-church' and Congregationalism may claim to be a not unimportant bridge between the high Protestant churches, Lutheran, Presbyterian and, if its inclusion be permitted, Anglican, and the popular Free Churches with their huge memberships, the Baptist churches, the Methodists of the present day, the Disciples of Christ, and smaller but influential bodies like the Society of Friends. That we look in both directions is proved by the fact that there are those in our midst who would emphasize our connections with one side or the other and that both can appeal to history in their support.[1] Congregationalists have strongly emphasized the freedom of the Spirit in ruling and guiding the Church, and, in modern times especially, have loved to quote the famous saying of John Robinson to the Pilgrims departing

[1] See J. S. Whale, *Christian Doctrine* (Cambridge University Press, 1941), and G. F. Nuttall, *The Holy Spirit and Puritanism* (Blackwell, 1946), and, for what is still the most illuminating discussion of the relation between the two sides, P. T. Forsyth's *Faith, Freedom and the Future*, 1912.

from Leyden to the New World that 'the Lord hath more light and truth yet to break forth out of His Holy Word'. In this, as in their emphasis on individual conviction and responsibility, they have shown their affinity with bodies of the 'spiritualizing' type, whether they be Baptist, Mennonite, or Quaker. On the other hand, most of the leading Congregational theologians, from the great John Owen onward, have insisted that the Church has a definite faith which can be defined in precise terms and a definite order which can be justified from Scripture. They have insisted, in P. T. Forsyth's phrase, that their freedom is a founded freedom, that it is from the Word, which is Jesus Christ as the Scriptures declare Him, that more light and truth are to break forth and not from the spirit of the age. They have also insisted that the true way of Congregationalism is not to reject but to restate and re-form classical church order in such a way that it becomes, not a hindrance, but the instrument of God's free rule in the Spirit over His people. This, of course, will be dealt with at greater length later, when we come to treat the essence of Congregationalism, but it is worth mentioning now because the fact that Congregationalism tries to hold these two traditions together in its own life gives it a greater ecumenical significance than might first appear. The 'spiritualizing' strain in the history of the Church has been inadequately represented in ecumenical discussion and its significance has been consequently under-estimated but this is likely to change in the future, especially as the attention of the World Council of Churches becomes more and more directed to the spiritual situation in America and among the Younger Churches.

What kind of an impact has Congregationalism made upon mankind? To look at it first externally, it clearly cannot claim to have established itself as one of the major forms of the Christian Church. It has had its glorious moments and has exercised an influence in many spheres greater than its numerical strength might suggest. But it can hardly maintain, even if it any longer desired to, that history is proving it to be that form of the Church for which all mankind is eagerly waiting. There have been times when it made such claims. Some of the architects of the New England experiment consciously believed that they were creating a church and a commonwealth purely reformed according to the Word of God which would be a decisive example to Old England and to the world of what a community living in covenant relation with God should be. They saw all history as a preparation for this event. God had sifted the nations to find the pure grain for this planting. With a courage and a sense of providential leading which can have few parallels in history they believed that, three thousand miles away from civilization across a wild ocean and in an unknown land, they were a city set upon a hill, whose light would shine over the whole earth. As Dr. Douglas Horton has emphasized again,[1] they were not Separatists in intention, who thought of themselves as a little flock, gathered out of the world to worship God in purity and peace, after the manner of innumerable other small sects in Christendom, including many others who followed them to America in later generations. They claimed to be the representatives of the true England, who hoped to convert those at home to their own point of view. The same large vision also inspired the Independents in the Army during the Great Rebellion, catching the imaginations of humble and unlettered laymen as well as those of the leaders. They saw a glimpse of an England of free and responsible men whose common life was ordered by the Spirit of the Word which spoke not only through a hierarchy but also through the whole company of believers. It found expression through the remarkable debates

[1] In his book, *Congregationalism: a Study in Church Polity* (Independent Press, London, 1952).

conducted by the Army on Putney Heath in 1647,[1] it was set forth in developed and cultivated theological form in the works of John Owen and others and made its most direct impact on the piety of the English people in the writings of John Bunyan.

The seventeenth century was, in terms of internal energy, purity and clarity of conviction and influence over great events, unquestionably the greatest period in the history of Congregationalism, both in England and America. Our churches have never reached such heights again. The full effect of the ultimate failure of Cromwell and the Independents to reform the church and common life of England has never been adequately appraised. Its consequences for the common life of England have been grave and would have been graver had it not been for the partial success of the Methodist Revival in the eighteenth century, because large and vigorous sections of the community were shut out from free participation in the public affairs and traditional culture of England. And its consequences for the internal life of Congregationalism were no less grave. It is true that it quickly won a partial toleration and that by now it has won a distinctive and established place in the life of the nation, but the process took over two hundred years and the price it has had to pay has been the surrender of its vision of reformation, a vision which it now finds hard to recapture even though the circumstances are more favourable for its realization.

American Congregationalism has not the same story of political and social failure to record. The 'godly commonwealth' of Massachusetts was well and truly founded and played an important, if not a decisive, part in the formation of the character and institutions of the American nation; who, in our own time, have achieved a power and influence in world

[1] Reprinted in *Puritanism and Liberty*, edited by A. S. P. Woodhouse (Dent, London, 1938).

affairs which even the bold dreams of the first colonists could hardly have envisaged. It is worth pondering upon the fact that that has happened and that it was from the impulse to form a 'godly commonwealth' that it originally sprang. There are some strains in the life even of modern America which make it not entirely fanciful to imagine it as the new England, the kind of country England might have become if the Independents had consolidated their triumph in the seventeenth century. Yet in America they must admit partial failure effectively to influence the nation and to be faithful to their own best insights. The New England influence in the development of America has been the strongest but it was not the only one. The size and the dynamic growth of the country have made that impossible and the influx of vast multitudes of immigrants of alien culture has produced a radically different situation even in New England itself from any which could have been envisaged in colonial times. Under the pressure of these events, the spirit and outlook of American Congregationalism itself have undergone a change and it is doubtful whether any of the early settlers returning now would recognize as much kinship with an American Congregational church of today as a seventeenth-century Independent would with a modern English Congregational church.

But if both major branches of Congregationalism have to confess to failure to maintain the level of the seventeenth century, that does not invalidate the fact that both can claim considerable achievements in the years which followed. The eighteenth century was, in its characteristic periods, not a time of outstanding accomplishment in the history of Congregationalism but it did produce Isaac Watts and Philip Doddridge. Too much may have been made of the fact that English Congregationalism, in contrast to Presbyterianism, resisted the inroads of Arianism despite its non-credalism, especially as American Congregationalism suffered so many losses to the same cause a little later, but it did succeed in keeping the faith and, when the Evangelical Revival came, it was in a good position to respond to it. Indeed, much of that coarsening of fibre and spiritual mediocrity which became only too characteristic of orthodox Dissent as the nineteenth century advanced was part of the price it had to pay for its very considerable evangelistic success, often with most unpromising material. The measure of success achieved by Congregationalism in baptizing and giving direction to the new middle classes produced by the Industrial Revolution has not always been fully acknowledged, especially in England. That some of them should have become smug, that their buildings and habits of worship should have occasionally displayed a *nouveau riche* lack of good taste, and that some of their political adventures, especially towards the end of the century, should have been ill-conceived is not, in the circumstances, surprising. As we shall see, a good deal of the blame for this must rest upon the shoulders of the Established Church. What is more remarkable is their success in reaching people who were not easily touched by the Established Church and the rich and full church and social life that they created for them. That they were effective schools of Christian nurture is proved, apart from anything else, by the fact that they quickly produced thier own sternest critics.

Nor should their positive achievements in this period be under-estimated. Congregational churches have been notable among English churches, and to some extent this is true of the English-speaking world in general, in their concern not only for personal experience of Christ but also for personal experience of Christ as the truth. It was this which enabled Congregational ministers and congregations to take the lead in trying to assimilate the findings of Biblical Criticism and to relate their understanding of the Gospel to the changed world-view produced by modern science. The defective grasp of the full meaning of Christian tradition displayed by some of their exponents led them to a weakened hold on what is distinctive in Christian faith which has left its mark on Congregationalism to this day, but that was partly a price paid for exceptional spiritual and intellectual courage, whose results have been of benefit to the whole Church. Although Congregationalism has suffered to the full from the trivialization which has overtaken most churches in recent generations, the sermon in a Congregational church still retains something of the character of a grapple with the deep things of God in the setting of human doubt, difficulty and need, on the basis of a careful exposition of Scripture. It is not an accident that Congregationalism has produced so many constructive theologians and that, among its ministers and people, on both sides of the Atlantic, its emphasis on education has been so strong.

The influence of Congregationalism on the common life of society is always in danger of being underrated because it is its genius to be at its weakest in metropolitan life and centralized organization and at its strongest in local communities. Thus few of the leaders of thought and action in our time are practising Congregationalists and very few of the numerous intellectually or socially prominent converts to Christian faith in our time are converted to Congregationalism. Yet many of these same people are the products of Congregational homes and have received the benefits of Congregational nurture. While these people receive little enough guidance from Congregationalism when they go out into the larger world, it is the Congregational church which is often the most effective spiritual and educational influence in the middle-class suburb or large industrial city in which they were brought up. Why this should be so and the problems which the answer raises for modern Congregationalism will be one of the main themes of our inquiry.

III

The Essence of Congregationalism

Congregationalists are very reluctant to define their distinctive beliefs with any degree of binding precision. Whether they are justified in this attitude and whether they can maintain it much longer in a situation where the various churches are seeking grounds for reunion is an open question but they make no secret of their reluctance and show little sign of abandoning it. They seem, indeed, to have absorbed something of the comprehensiveness and toleration of ambiguity of the Church of England in this respect. While they have, of necessity, been much more definite on matters of order than of faith, even on these there have been important differences between one church and another, and no authoritative statements about what constitutes Congregational polity are available. On the other hand, Congregationalists, in contrast to many other Free Church bodies, have, throughout their history, been unusually forthcoming in making statements concerning their faith and order, for which they have always been careful to claim no more than declaratory authority. Despite their emphasis on freedom of interpretation, there has, in fact, been a very large degree of unity of belief and practice on their part throughout their history. It is not difficult, therefore, to specify in a general way what the distinctive position of Congregationalism is, even though it might be very difficult to seek to enforce that interpretation upon any Congregationalist who happened to disagree.

The Essence of Congregationalism

The various classical statements of Congregationalism, the Savoy Declaration of 1658 and the Declaration of Faith and Order made at the founding of the Congregational Union of England and Wales in 1831, and in America the Cambridge Platform of 1648 and the Kansas City Declaration of 1911, indicate strongly the general affinity which Congregationalism holds with other Reformed churches, both in the uncompromising Calvinism which was characteristic of it in the seventeenth century and in the severe modification which that Calvinism underwent in more recent times. The chief explicit differences have, in fact, been in the realm of polity rather than of belief. It is well known that the framers of the Savoy Declaration expressed their whole-hearted assent to the doctrinal sections of the Westminster Confession, which was formulated by the predominantly Presbyterian Westminster Assembly of Divines, and contented themselves with adding their Independent view of church polity as a supplement to that Confession.[1] Yet, inevitably, these differences over polity have had subtle implications for their approach to doctrines, even if not always to their explicit formulations, and a characteristic emphasis and spirit of Congregationalism emerge over wider matters than those of polity. It shares with the sects their conception of the Church as a gathered community of believers who have been called out of the world by Christ and who have responded to that call with a deliberate act of committal of themselves to Him. It is also at one with them in giving concrete expression to the priesthood of all believers by insisting on the right and duty of all members of the church in good standing to share in its government. But it differs from them in having a much more developed and conscious sense of the Church as the Body of Christ. And while it is at one with

[1] And Congregationalists have frequently pointed out that they could assent to thirty-six of the Thirty-Nine Articles, which is, perhaps, a better score than that achieved by many Anglicans in these days.

the other Reformed churches in its resistance to Erastianism and Prelacy and its insistence upon 'the crown rights of the Redeemer' in His Church, its clear recognition of the primacy of the Gospel over the Church has given it a less rigid and more flexible conception of church organization than that often evinced by Presbyterian bodies. If a slogan were required to pick out what is distinctive of Congregationalism among the churches with which it has most kinship, that which would probably receive the most widespread approval would be the word 'Freedom'. But, in order to see that in its proper context, most Congregationalists would want to add, as they frequently do, the words 'Faith' and 'Fellowship' as expressing realities equally fundamental in their conception of their church.

Like most popular slogans, however, 'Faith, Freedom, and Fellowship' conceal as much as they reveal and many of the debates in modern Congregationalism have, in effect, turned on the kind of meaning which they should carry. There have been, and on many points there still are, sharp disagreements between Congregationalists about how they should be interpreted. It would be vain to pretend that what follows would win universal acceptance as an attempt to expound their meaning. But, while account must be taken of such disagreements, there is more of a common mind among Congregationalists as to their meaning than would have seemed possible thirty or even ten years ago. Many might prefer to put it differently, but it would be surprising if more than a minority of Congregationalists, especially in England, disagreed radically with what follows.

In regard to the key-word 'faith', Congregationalists have always strongly insisted upon their evangelical character. Only in the period of the New Theology controversy before 1914 and in the unsettled decade after 1918 has there been any significant number who have shown serious hesitation on this point despite a widespread impression to the contrary. The faith of Congregationalists is the faith of Scripture, as interpreted in the light of its assured central content, Jesus Christ. In the seventeenth century, it would hardly have occurred to any Independents to have thought otherwise than that. In the eighteenth century in England and in the nineteenth in America, the challenge of Unitarianism had to be directly faced, but those who wished to retain the name of Congregationalist were not the Unitarians. When the full impact of Biblical Criticism and of the theological modernism which partly arose out of it was experienced in the early twentieth century, there were few even among the modernists themselves who would have challenged it. The ultimate justification given until very recently for Congregational polity was that it was demonstrably closer to the New Testament church than that of any other body. The classic Congregational objection to the use of the creeds in worship or as tests of membership was not that their acceptance presented the believer with intellectual difficulties but that they could not claim the same measure of authority as Scripture and that it was wrong to impose tests on men which were other than those given by God Himself. Whether this attitude was justified is not now our concern. Even when many in Congregationalism did move away from the older orthodoxy, in the heyday of theological liberalism, they did not do so by disparaging or ignoring Scripture but by claiming that their interpretation was more faithful to Scripture critically interpreted than was that of the old orthodoxy, and several of their most eloquent exponents were Biblical scholars. Although there is probably less Fundamentalism in Congregationalism than in any other major Protestant church, Congregationalists are 'people of the book' no less than Presbyterians, Methodists, and Baptists.

Congregationalists in recent times have not always recognized this as clearly as they might but, in fact, their history and their present existence make very little sense without it. What is it which has kept the loosely-organized Congregational churches together, throughout the centuries and across the oceans, if it has not been the fact that the Bible has been open in their midst, and that together they have sought God's will from it, as the living Christ declares it? It is true that, once churches are firmly established, common *mores* and ordinary connections of family and organization help to hold them together. These factors operate in Congregationalism as they do elsewhere, but they tend to be weaker in our churches than they are among most of the other smaller churches of the world. It is hard to see how Congregationalism could have held together in the way it has with its free outlook and loose organization, especially amidst the confusion of the last half-century, if its members had not ultimately possessed a common responsibility to a Lord who is clearly recognizable as the Christ of the New Testament.

In this, of course, they are fortunately no different from numerous other Christian churches and to insist on it may seem to some to be labouring the obvious. But it needs to be emphasized because, partly as a result of their unusual attitude towards creeds, many Congregationalists themselves have not fully realized the extent to which their whole life depends on an act of faith in Christ. Their very non-credalism, as some of them choose to call it, and their reluctance to tie themselves by any kind of legal restraints from following the Spirit wherever it may lead, make them more completely dependent on this faith than almost any other church. In our next chapter, we shall have occasion to face some of the implications of this fact for the kind of situation in which Congregationalism finds itself today.

Similarly, the word 'fellowship' is also used to cover many different things and has frequently been given a sentimental connotation which makes many people distrust it, an objection which can nowadays also be levelled at the more modern catchword, 'community'. But the word *koinonia* is, after all, a great New Testament word and there is an important reality lying behind the choice of 'fellowship' to describe part of what is distinctive in Congregationalism.

Congregationalism is often taken to represent the apotheosis of religious individualism. The use of its synonym 'Independent', helps to confirm this impression. And it has to be admitted, as we shall see, that misconceptions of the nature of Christian freedom and inability adequately to express the relation between the local church and the great Church have sometimes given some substance to it. Yet, in its essence, Congregationalism stands for the very reverse of religious individualism. For no church order insists more specifically on the fact that there can be no such thing as a solitary Christian. To be a Christian means to belong to the company of the Lord's people, the Church, and to belong to the Church, Congregationalists say, does not mean to belong to the Church in general but to a particular congregation. It means to enter into communion with one's fellow-Christians in the most immediate and inescapable way, in the local church. As John Owen, the great Independent divine of the seventeenth century, puts it, 'I will try you here,' said Christ, 'I require this of you indispensably to love all the saints, all believers, all my disciples. You shall not need to say you must go far, this way or that, for objects. I appoint you to such an order as wherein you shall have continual immediate objects of all that love which I require of you. . . . Let none, then, pretend that they love the brethren in general, and love the people of God, and love the saints, while their love is not fervently exercised towards all those that are in the same church with them.' And to love means to think with and live with and act with the local church. As is often pointed out in Congregational churches, the meaning of that much-quoted saying of our Lord 'Where two or three are gathered together in my name, there am I in the midst', is not that any little casual group who gather together and invoke the name of Christ by that act constitute themselves a church. It is that more than one person is needed before there can be an ecclesiastical quorum, that the church does not come alive as a church unless at least two or three are gathered together because, until that happens, Christ will not appear in the midst. In so far as it is true that John Milton was an Independent who belonged to a church with one member, John Milton, he denied the fundamental principle of Independency. Nothing shocks a Congregationalist in Roman Catholic practice more than the spectacle of a priest celebrating a solitary mass.

It is this emphasis on the particularity of the Church, much more than its emphasis on freedom, which is, perhaps, the greatest contribution of Congregationalism to the life of the whole Church. It takes the Church seriously, not by developing a 'high' doctrine about it whose character may be largely symbolic, nor by magnifying the power and dignity of the hierarchy in such a way that the weakness of the believing fellowship is concealed by its strength, but by insisting that every believer must come to terms with it in its most concrete form, the local company of Christ's people gathered together into church order.

There are several reasons why Congregationalism has failed to retain the loyalty of some of its ablest and best-educated children in our own time and has not attracted the same number of distinguished converts to its ranks that both Rome and Canterbury can claim, and some of those reasons point to serious weaknesses in its life. But there are other reasons which reflect, not its weakness, but its strength, and it is important that they should be frankly recognized. 'Presbyterianism', said Charles II, in a notorious phrase, 'is no religion for a gentleman,' and that is even more true of Congregationalism if to be a gentleman, as it apparently was for Charles II, is to regard oneself as of a superior order of being to one's fellow-men and entitled to limitless privileges. Should one be a person accustomed to command and to receive deference because of one's exceptional accomplishment, wealth, or social standing, should one possess religious desires or difficulties of a highly specialized character, it is an exercise of great humility to accept membership of a Congregational church. It is often put forward as a great virtue of Roman Catholicism in particular that in its churches rich and poor, wise and simple, conventional and unconventional, can all be found worshipping together unselfconsciously in the same way. Up to a point it is indeed a virtue, and Congregational and other Free Churches can learn much from the hierarchical coherence and liturgical objectivity which make it possible. But, when this pleasing fact is used to buttress large claims of universality, it becomes pertinent to inquire how much concreteness is given in the Roman Catholic Church to the demand of Christ that his members should love all the saints. And the word 'saints' is used here as John Owen used it, in the Biblical sense of the ordinary body of believers in the local church, as distinct from those figures of outstanding spiritual quality who are not elevated to the rank of sainthood until they have ceased to be members of any local church. It is not hard for the Guards officer and the distinguished novelist and the artistic peeress to hear Mass in the same church as the Irish labourer and the elementary school-teacher's wife and the secretary of the funeral club, if that is their sole association. It becomes more complicated if they are also expected to attend church meetings and serve teas at church social gatherings together and send their children to the same Sunday schools. No one familiar with the facts would want to idealize the record of Congregationalism in this respect. It has, often enough, settled down complacently to be a class church, even if its class has not been the most rigidly exclusive, and has unconsciously shut out many from its membership simply because they did not fit in with the 'Congregationalist way of doing things', without raising the question whether Christ would have debarred them. But it can claim, as against those denominations who are, perhaps, too ready to glamorize their alleged universality, that it has made a determined attempt to create a genuine Christian fellowship in the place where it matters most and where it is most difficult and costly, in the particular local congregation.

The place where the life in fellowship of a Congregational church is meant to find its focus is in the church meeting. The church meeting, a distinctive element in Congregational polity, is a regular meeting of all members of the church in good standing in which, presided over by the minister and guided by their deacons, they take counsel together and reach decisions concerning all the affairs of their own congregation, both spiritual and temporal. How the church meeting is related to the worship of the church, what its powers and characteristic activities are and whether, in its present form, it fulfils all that is claimed for it, are questions which will be looked at in later sections. What needs to be made clear at this stage is that the element of fellowship receives its recognition in the very structure of a Congregational church. Not only does Congregationalism insist that a church should be a family, it also gives the church an organ of family responsibility. The church meeting is not a club of the like-minded, who frame rules to suit their own convenience and according to whims of their own. It is a solemn assembly of the people of God in a particular place, who meet together before God, to consider together, in the light of the Word which is preached and on the basis of their sacramental fellowship with Christ, how they may discern and obey the Lord's will for themselves as His people in that place. It is the place where the fellowship with each other of all who love the Lord Jesus Christ is, to use a favourite phrase of John Owen's, gathered into church order.

The phrase 'gathering into church order' is worth dwelling upon both because it indicates that those who hold to the concept of the 'gathered church' have a very definite concept of church order, which is closely allied to that of the 'gathered church', and also because it gives an indication of how Congregationalists and, indeed, most other Reformed churches, conceive the way in which particular churches came into being. Christ calls each person individually to be His follower. His normal way of doing that may be through the visible family of His people but His Spirit is now shed abroad through the world and His ways of doing so are not limited to the activity of the visible churches. But, when Christ calls, He brings the company of His saints with Him. Each individual is called by name, but he is not called in isolation. He is called to join the family of the Church and to do so in the way which has most reality and concreteness in terms of his life on earth. He has to live as a Christian in his dealings with all men but with 'those that are of the household of faith' he has the duty of living 'in church order'. This, as can be seen, is much more than a matter of dealing with the business and organizational sides of the church's institutional existence. It is a matter of a different set of personal relationships from those which are possible with unbelievers. A personal responsibility rests upon each of its members to ensure that their life together has this 'church order'. They have to make arrangements for the Word to be preached to them by a minister competent to do so, and for the Sacraments to be administered according to God's ordinance. They have to ensure that they are in effective contact with other churches in the Great Church. And they have, together, to exhort and admonish each other to maintain a Christian walk and conversation as the Lord's people in their own place. In this task, as we shall see, ministers and other officers have special responsibilities, but the general responsibility for its fulfilment rests upon the whole body of the church membership. Whether the institution of the church meeting as it is established in present-day English Congregationalism is the best instrument for fulfilling it is a question which is open to profitable debate,[1] especially in relation to its ability adequately to express the communion of the churches with each other, but that an organ something like it is a necessity in the life of a Reformed church would seem to be undeniable. The doctrine of the priesthood of all believers, together with its correlative notions of justification by faith and the freedom of the Christian man, would seem to demand it. To argue that it exposes the church to the dangers of an ill-informed democracy is only to show that the full import of those doctrines has not been grasped. Congregationalism stands or falls by the conviction that the fellowship must find its expression in the very structure of church order.

The third popular watchword of Congregationalism, 'Freedom', is that which is the most frequently invoked of all and that which lends itself to the greatest variety of interpretation. All Congregationalists agree that their churches have a special contribution to make to the expression of the Christian belief in freedom but they often disagree sharply over what they mean by it. The brilliant and prophetic book of P. T. Forsyth, *Faith, Freedom and the Future*, which was written a generation ago has posed the issues, at least from one point of view, in terms which are hardly less relevant today than when it was first written. All Congregationalists would be at one in

[1] See the discussions of it which are necessary in those Younger Churches which are in process of being fully established, in *Congregationalism Plus* by Dr. Norman Goodall (Independent Press, London, 1953).

insisting on the right of the Church to rule in its own house, that Christ might speak through His Church, and would deny the right of the State or any other power to interfere in its affairs. In this, however, they would also find that the majority of their fellow-Christians would now agree with them, even though some have not yet been able to extricate themselves from embarrassing entanglements which they inherited, and others have to fight for their life against dictators. It is in regard to the Church's freedom in relation to standards of belief that anything distinctive emerges in the position of Congregationalism in these days. Classic Congregationalism, as Forsyth pointed out, represented a fusion of Calvinism with the emphasis on the free leading of the Spirit which was characteristic of Anabaptism. It was a church of the Word, but it was also a church which believed that God had more light and truth to break forth from His Word and gave gifts to His people for the discernment and declaration of that light and truth. His people must, therefore, be careful not to allow themselves to be so set in the ways of a rigid orthodoxy that they refuse to follow the Spirit into new ways. Further, although this is a notion which has received explicit formulation only in more recent times, since Christ in the Spirit demands to be received as the truth and requires 'truth in the inward parts', the genuine, unreserved commitment of the mind, the possibility must be honestly faced that He is not the truth. No challenge to faith can be evaded by the pious invocation of the authority of tradition. There must be freedom of inquiry in the church as a condition of being able to vindicate the freedom of God in His revelation.

The danger, which has often become an actuality in modern times, of this bold insistence on freedom is, of course, that men misuse their liberty. It is always difficult to discern the spirits whether they be of Christ and, unless men have a firmly-grounded knowledge of who Christ is and what the fruits of His Spirit are, they can easily slip into following the spirit of the age or the spirit of their own particular sect instead of Christ. And when they have followed these spirits so far that they have lost sight of Christ, it is possible for them to come to believe that their attachment to them is greater than their attachment to Him. Because of this, Congregationalists have come more and more in recent years to insist that the freedom they claim is, in Forsyth's words, a founded freedom. It is a freedom which arises from the experience of God in Christ as the Scriptures declare Him and as the Spirit-guided Church throughout the ages has known Him. It is a freedom which maintains itself by keeping close to Christ, whose service is perfect freedom, because the Gospel is that it is only those who are in Christ who find their true nature as men and, through that, their power of self-determination in accordance with their true ends. How this is related to what is commonly called freedom of thought and the authority of the Bible and the creeds is clearly a matter of great importance when Congregationalism's relation to the ecumenical movement is considered. To its more detailed discussion we must now turn.

IV

Faith and Freedom

It is appropriate that faith and freedom be discussed together because, in the history of Congregationalism, they have been most intimately linked and the relation between them has always provoked vigorous discussion concerning the nature of both. It is only occasionally that Congregationalists have gone as far as some modern Unitarians in virtually declaring their faith to be not in Christ but in religious freedom and in showing more interest in proclaiming their freedom of inquiry and their right to follow their consciences wherever they may lead than in stating the conclusions to which this exercise has led them. But the influence of an attitude of that kind has spread widely throughout Congregationalism in the course of the present century, with the result that much Congregational teaching about both faith and freedom has been less clear and constructive than might reasonably be expected.

It has already been pointed out that the ambivalent attitude displayed by Congregationalists on the subject of freedom has served partly to conceal, even from their members, the extent to which Congregational churches are, in fact, founded on an act of belief as decisive and far-reaching as that taken by any other church, an act of belief in the lordship of Jesus Christ and His reign in the Church through the Holy Spirit. How this act of belief is related to the attitudes commonly displayed by Congregationalists in relation to creeds will have to be discussed later in this chapter, but a study of all major Congregational documents until about fifty years ago will make clear the way in which they take their stand upon it. Even within the last fifty years, it is worth noting that no official Congregational statement in regard to matters of faith has deviated from it. It is true that many Congregationalists within the last couple of generations, though it is doubtful whether they ever constituted more than a minority, have been influenced by a temporizing attitude towards the lordship of Christ. The period of the New Theology before the 1914 war and of Modernism in the 1920's represented the peak of this influence, which has been far more widespread in America than in England. But, even at these times, the attitude of hesitation in relation to the lordship of Christ has been more characteristic than that of rejection. Few modernist Congregationalists reached the degree of explicit statement found in a book like Frank Lenwood's *Jesus, Lord or Leader?*[1] and some have doubted whether that book accurately expressed what was the real working faith of its author, who was a man of deep and sacrificial personal piety. That this was a passing mood rather than a revolutionary change of outlook which overtook Congregationalism is proved by the fact that today it would be hard to think of any prominent and influential Congregational minister who would not want strenuously to assert that Congregational churches were based on a belief in the lordship of Christ.

We have already mentioned why it is important that this point should be brought out. It is not merely to reassure other denominations that Congregationalism, despite its queer stop in the mind about creeds and binding statements of faith, is as overtly Christian as the rest, although it would not be unreasonable on their part to demand such reassurance. It is also that Congregationalism must admit that it cannot make much sense to itself unless it recognizes frankly that this is the

[1] Constable, London, 1928.

belief by which it lives and which controls its whole conception of the Church. What marks off the Church of Jesus Christ from any society which might gather together because it is interested in religious matters in a general way is its belief that its life is controlled and directed by Jesus Christ, to whom the Scriptures bear faithful witness and who is present as an active power in the midst through the Spirit. This is the very essence of the Church's being. The whole purpose of church order is to express and safeguard the continuing lordship of Christ in the believing community, so that it remains a fellowship of Christ's people and does not dissolve into the world about it. In seeing this, Congregationalism is, of course, at one with other churches, especially with the other churches of the Reformation. The uniqueness of Congregationalism historically has consisted in the extent to which it has maintained that the present rule of Christ in His Church through His Spirit is the principle of church order. The procedure of public worship and the importance of the sermon as an attempt to listen to the voice of the living Christ in the midst, the emphasis on the church meeting as the gathering in which all members are able to exercise their spiritual gifts so that Christ should not be shut out from the church simply because only the minister of the Word is allowed to speak, the insistence on the 'crown rights of the Redeemer' in His Church as forbidding any external and non-spiritual control of the Church, all these underline the way in which Congregationalism makes nonsense of itself unless it recognizes its dependence on this belief.

Other churches can reasonably demand of Congregationalism that it straighten out its thinking on this matter in ecumenical conversation. That it is not too difficult a task and that it does not involve any startling change of attitude in Congregationalism is proved by the fact that Congregational churches, in Canada and prospectively in the United States, have entered into unions with churches which have accepted creeds and confessions and all Congregational churches have joined the World Council of Churches, which lays great stress on the fact that its basis of membership is belief in Jesus Christ as God and Saviour. The difficulties which Congregationalists have experienced with the central articles of Christian belief in the last couple of generations have not differed in kind or degree from those experienced by members of many other churches. What can be argued, however, is that the attitude towards creeds, notably the Apostles' and Nicene Creeds, which has become conventional in modern Congregationalism, has made it harder than it need be for Congregationalism frankly to face the issues involved in belief in the central articles of Christian belief, notably that in relation to the divinity of our Lord, and have encouraged some Congregational churches to provide a haven for ministers from other churches who wished to avoid facing these issues.

It may seem tendentious thus to describe as a weakness what many Congregationalists may still regard as a source of strength in their life and witness but while, as we shall see, some beneficial results have come from the Congregational insistence on freedom of inquiry into the basis of Christian belief, it is doubtful whether they could be placed to the credit of our alleged non-credalism. After all, the traditional Congregational objection to creeds as tests of membership was, in a sense a formal one.[1] It was not that they did not believe the creeds. Most Congregationalists throughout history would have been horrified at such an idea. But their sense of the supreme and overriding authority of Scripture

[1] And it is important to realize that many Congregationalists did not consider that their use in this way was in any sense improper. Even so representative a Congregationalist of the first half of the twentieth century as J. D. Jones of Bournemouth used to maintain the custom of having church members recite the Apostles' Creed on being received into membership.

was such, and their anxiety to refute Catholic teaching concerning the authority of tradition so great, that they wished to accept nothing which might deflect men from going to Scripture as the fount of all doctrine. They would have agreed that, in substance, the creeds were congruous with the central message of Scripture and were documents of great importance. Their concern was to preserve the authority of God in His revelation.

When modernist theologians arose, however, their claim was that there existed a simple body of teaching given by the man Jesus, whose life of self-sacrificing devotion was an example to us all, which was quickly elaborated into a great dogmatic structure by the apostolic church. This process was carried further by the church of the first four centuries, reaching its climax in the complicated Christological formulations of the Nicene Creed and the harsh exclusiveness of the *Quicunque Vult.* What the modernists wished to do was, in effect, to reject the teaching of the apostolic church and to replace it by their own conception of the 'Jesus of History', and they found in the qualifications which Congregationalism made about the authority of the creeds a convenient loophole for allowing them to do so. But this was a misuse of those qualifications and led them to a position which those who had originally made them would have been the first to repudiate. For, quite apart from the large question of whether it is possible to recreate a 'Jesus of history' who is radically different in character from the Christ of apostolic faith, its effect was to allow the modernists to evade the challenge which the creeds presented to their understanding of the Gospel.

For, after all, what is the purpose of the creeds? It is not a mark of intellectual honesty but the reverse to do what often has been done, to describe them always with an emotionally coloured adjective such as 'outworn' or 'stuffy' without considering carefully what they claim to do and to say. Intellectual honesty demands not that one strains every nerve to sound enlightened and up-to-date but that every effort is made to understand an idea which may be presumed to have a claim upon one's attention before it is rejected. That is peculiarly true in the case of the creeds because their intention is to ensure that the considerations which they emphasize must always be borne in mind by anyone who claims to define Christian truth. They do not put themselves forward as exhaustive statements of the whole of Christian truth, although they may sometimes have been treated like that, but as acts of witness on the part of accredited representatives of the churches of their own day, gathered together in solemn council, to the truth of certain central Christian affirmations. The concern of the creeds is to insist that it is the considered judgment of those who framed them that no man whose business it is to think of these things can be a Christian believer who does not maintain and safeguard against misinterpretation those truths concerning the Trinity and the person of our Lord with which they deal. They do their utmost to ensure that all generations of Christians who came after them should face this challenge directly and try to meet it.

Now it is true, as Congregationalism rightly insists, that the acceptance of the creeds should not be automatic in any church. The realities of which they speak cannot be personally appropriated simply because they are in the creeds. Since, as the Thirty-nine Articles of the Church of England themselves say, it is possible for a General Council to err, it is conceivable that the authors of the creeds were wrong in some particular. Further, it is not only permissible but desirable and inevitable that a living church should try to express what the creeds expressed in the language of their day in terms of the very different language of its own day. In a sense this is what every piece of systematic theological work tries to do. What is culpable is to ignore the witness of the creeds or to pretend that the issues with which they confront us are not fundamental and need not trouble us unduly. That is not intellectual honesty. It is an act of obscurantism, produced by an insensitive lack of historical sympathy and an inadequate humility in the presence of the witness of our fathers in the faith. It is also an unbrotherly act towards that great mass of Christians in other churches, the overwhelming majority of whom venerate the creeds and use them regularly in their worship. The freedom which many Congregationalists have claimed in relation to the creeds in modern times has not been the proper freedom to scrutinize them vigorously in the light of Scripture and of the history of the ways of God with men from their day to this. It has been a freedom to ignore the creeds as not contributing anything significant to our understanding of the Gospel. This has encouraged Congregationalists in the radically mistaken notion that it is possible to have Congregational churches which have not made up their minds where they stand in relation to the lordship of Christ, producing an uncertainty and confusion of belief which have made it harder for them to discern the will of God for them in the changing circumstances of our time.

Other churches have a right, therefore, to demand that Congregationalists clear their minds on this matter and deal honestly with themselves and with others in relation to creeds and confessions. Whatever be our precise attitude to the so-called ecumenical creeds of the first four centuries, and let it be agreed that that question still requires more examination than can be given it in this short discussion, Congregationalists cannot be allowed any longer to assume that they solve any problems by refusing to make up their minds about the need for credal statements as such. We are just as much committed to faith in the lordship of Christ as other churches are. The fact that we may allow a greater liberality of interpretation of what that means than some others do may be wise, but it does not exempt us from the necessity of drawing a line somewhere, and our hesitation over doing so earns us a reputation not for catholicity of temper but for irresponsibility. Such irresponsibility may be engaging and even beneficial for a brief season in the life of a church, as it can be in the life of an individual, but once the ecumenical question is seriously raised it becomes manifestly culpable.

This is very far from implying that Congregationalism in the last couple of generations, when all churches have passed through a period of great confusion and change, has been consistently on the wrong track. On the contrary, we have constantly emphasized that it is very significant that a large section, and that by no means the least influential, has not been guilty of this evasion. Because it faced this issue while maintaining a firm grasp on the authentic Congregational teaching concerning freedom, it has done as much as any other group in Christendom to point the way to a richer understanding of the purpose of God for His people today. P. T. Forsyth held a place of great influence among Congregationalists and, although he suffered the fate of many other prophetic leaders of being more widely appreciated after his death than in his lifetime, he was never without powerful support even in the darkest days. And it is of great significance that, although Congregationalism has been more shaken in its grasp of central Christian realities by the strain of recent times than most other denominations, this was partly because it had the courage to expose itself to them the more boldly. As a concomitant of this, it shows very clear signs today of recovering from any damage they have caused the more rapidly. Some churches still have to come to terms honestly with the findings of Biblical Criticism. The fact that Congregationalism, like those churches closely related to it, has done so and renewed its assurance of the truth of the apostolic faith is likely to make its position and influence all the stronger in the years which are before us.

Yet the fact that they have been so deeply affected by the less constructive aspects of the modernist period has lessons to teach Congregationalists from which they, and other churches like them, still have much to learn. It is difficult for the present generation of Congregationalists, of whom the present writer is one, to learn those lessons aright because they are still too near that period to look at it in a wide enough context, but this is one of the places at which the more ample vision provided by the ecumenical movement can be of assistance.

The intellectual situation out of which the modernist movements of the late nineteenth and early twentieth centuries arose has frequently enough been described but nothing like as much attention has been paid to the social and religous situations, yet those are at least equally important. For example, the fact that, on the European continent and to some extent in the Church of England, modernism arose as a movement of intellectuals in old-established churches, whereas in Free Church Britain and America it arose out of pietist evangelicalism of a popular character, has never been given sufficient weight in evaluating its significance. More than an ocean separates Harnack from Shailer Matthews, and there is a decisive cultural difference between Renan's *Life of Jesus* and Bruce Barton's *The Man Nobody Knows*. The modernist movement in Congregationalism owes far more to the reaction against popular evangelicalism than it does to the direct influence of continental scholars.

This is proved by the kind of attack which P. T. Forsyth, who was in constant encounter with it, made upon it. He always complained that, whereas modernism asserted that it was deeply influenced by German scholarship, it was only some aspects of German scholarship to which it paid attention, and it ignored the large number of those who spoke in different accents from its own. It was as a popular movement, a prevailing mood, rather than a consistent system, that he had to fight against it and he constantly rebuked it for its provincialism, its spiritual amateurism, its lack of the public and the historic sense. The extent of the impact of modernism of this kind on Congregationalism has been partly minimised both because those Congregational spokesmen who have had most influence in other churches, Dale, Forsyth, Manning, Whale, Micklem, Dodd, have belonged to a different school and because the effect of pietist evangelicalism on Victorian and immediately post-Victorian Congregationalism has been seriously under-estimated.

The direct influence of the forms of pietist evangelicalism which are mentioned in the history books, Methodism, the Evangelical Revival, the Great Awakening, was not as great or immediate on Congregationalism as it was on the life of some other churches, although it was certainly considerable. But the influence of the continued revivals of broadly evangelical character which went on throughout the nineteenth century was very much greater and in two important, though unobtrusive, ways. First, the influence was very great among the laity and especially those in the smaller churches. Secondly, many who joined Congregational churches came to them from churches of strongly evangelical character, so that the religious experience which was the background of their lives was of this kind. All this was particularly true of the last great revival which swept through the churches, that of Moody and Sankey. This came at the very time when the new knowledge brought by Biblical Criticism and the new outlook engendered by modern science were gathering to a flood and beginning seriously to affect the popular consciousness.

The chief strength of this evangelicalism lay in the fact that it produced an intense and specific religious experience which encouraged a deep personal devotion on the part of the believer to our Lord. The whole Church is profoundly in its debt because it has undoubtedly proved itself the most effective evangelistic agency of modern times. But its limitations were grave, particularly for the time in which it had to live. It was excessively individualistic. Its conception of the spiritual life was concentrated too exclusively upon seeking to induce stereotyped forms of conversion experience. It had little sense of the Christian past. It had hardly a glimmering of the possibility of making the intellectual life a sphere of Christian discipleship. And in its laudable desire to reach the maximum number of people in the shortest possible time it became a pioneer in the techniques of mass suggestion which have been put to such sinister uses by the advertisers and politicians and entertainers of our time. Its great, overriding virtue was that it made many people Christians who were not Christians before and put them into circulation among the churches.

The effect of this movement upon its more sensitive children, or upon its children's children, was to give them strong religious impulses, largely focalized upon the person of our Lord, but very little intellectual equipment to meet the challenges to faith of their own very disturbed times and very few resources for developing their cultural life in a Christian direction. The result has become familiar. Some took the way of making a rigid separation between their life of personal faith and their secular activities, producing such well-known types as the Fundamentalist doctor who accepts his standards of professional thought and conduct as given by the society in which he finds himself without ever bringing a Christian judgment to bear on them. Others fled to a form of Christianity as unlike that in which they had been brought up as they could find, Catholicism. Others again took the way of rejecting Christian faith altogether. But not a few became modernists. This was a far more creative move than the rest but their background left the modernists with little defence against the new dogmas promulgated by secular philosophers or against the glamour of secular culture. The result was that their attempt to interpret the Gospel in terms of 'modern thought' often became little more than an attempt to find some justification for their own personal faith in Jesus while they accepted teachings about the nature of reality in the world around them which appeared to contradict that faith. This meant not only that they lost their grip on what was distinctive in Christian revelation but also that they failed in their effort to make the Gospel relevant to the modern world. They had capitulated so completely, in their minds if not in their hearts, to the spirit of the age that they were unable to discern the spirits whether they be of Christ, and when the spirit of the age changed they found it hard to follow it. Although in the Social Gospel movement it had its moments of genuine prophetic power, Modernism quickly lost its prophetic quality and it was left to Catholicism and to revived Reformation Protestantism to give Christians the intellectual resources to interpret the will of God for the cultural crisis of our time.

What is important, however, is not to rehearse this familiar story at length again but to ask what lessons it has to teach Congregationalism for the future. The modernist episode in its history has shown it the dangers of a conception of freedom which is not a founded freedom, founded in an act of faith in God revealed in Christ as the Scriptures declare Him and as the Great Church throughout the world has known him. This is not a matter simply of our possessing a more explicit relation to the creeds and requiring more definite commitment to the central articles of Christian belief, although we might well do more in that direction. The experience of the Church of England in the same period as that which we have described indicates that these can have no more than a restraining and mitigating effect. It is a matter of possessing a clear understanding, which is driven home by the whole life and witness of the Church, of what the Gospel and the Church are and of what the place is of our own particular denomination in our own particular time in the setting of God's purpose for His people. Only thus can a church venture freely into the unknown trusting to God's Spirit, because only if it is in that place can a church be confident that it is acting in conformity with that Spirit.

When Christians speak of the Church, they should not mean merely their own local church or their own denomination or even the body of Christian believers throughout the world in their own day. They should mean the whole company of God's people, as they have existed from the beginning until now. All who have borne the name of Christ are His people, whoever they be and wherever they have lived in time. He dwells with His people in His Spirit, who guides them in the knowledge of His will. And that will is one will. It will have varying applications in constantly changing situations, but Christ does not contradict Himself. To know His will in one particular situation requires at least a general knowledge of His will for mankind, as given pre-eminently in the revelation to which Scripture testifies but also as expressed in the history of the whole Church. If that is true in a measure for the individual, it is true to a much greater degree for a church. No church can clearly discern God's will for itself unless it sees itself as part of the whole and as having a distinctive responsibility to the rest of the whole. The relation of this to the ecumenical movement will be clear. Its significance for our understanding of the function of the ministry in Congregationalism will be part of the theme of the next chapter.

Now it is true, of course, that many churches can be

shackled by the past and the witness of churches like Congregationalism is needed to warn them against this grave danger. But no church can ignore the past. All of us, whether as individuals or churches, are the children of our parents and no greater illusion exists than to imagine that we have successfully emancipated ourselves from their influence simply by saying that we have. Those who imagine that they have done so have emancipated only the tops of their minds and are unconsciously conditioned in all kinds of ways by their past. Here the findings of modern psychology have drawn attention very strikingly to what is a common experience. No one is more obviously affected by his parents than the self-consciously rebellious young person who has in a 'progressive' and 'enlightened' way ostentatiously broken off external associations with his parents and their attitudes and mode of life. This is not to say that all men are inevitably and completely conditioned by their parents but it is to say that the only way to make a significant decision which is a genuine exercise of freedom in relation to the past is to recognize the extent of one's dependence upon it and the precise places where emancipation is possible as well as desirable. That is true of life in general but it is peculiarly true of churches because of the special relation in which they stand towards particular revealing events in the past and because of the continuity of experience which arises through their possession of a common living Spirit.

It was their failure to see this which was the great weakness of the modernists and, although there were other influences at work in Congregationalism, the confusion in the minds of Congregationalists about the relation between faith and freedom allowed their ideas to spread more quickly and more dangerously through Congregational churches than through many others. To them their determination to relate the Gospel to the new currents of thought which were moving through their time seemed to be creative and liberating and courageous and in many ways it indeed was. But, because the original experience of the Christian faith from which they started was so limited and they found it so easy to point out its inadequacies, they failed to see what immense resources were available to them in the thought and experience of the Christian ages for meeting the challenges of their own time. Their own roots were not deep, they lacked the humility to learn from other churches whose roots were deeper, and fellow-Christians in their own and other churches who might have helped them to learn did not always handle them with enough patience and sympathy. The result was that, so far from encouraging their followers in courageous and independent thought and action, they tended only to confuse them and led them to embrace either a new dogmatism of a contentless freedom of thought or to settle down to a shallow mediocrity of outlook, which looked askance at any idea which was unfamiliar or disturbing.

That this last should be the end-product of modernism in Congregationalism may be ironical but there is no doubt that this shallow mediocrity is the most characteristic weakness of Congregationalism today, both in Britain and the U.S.A., and that it flourishes most vigorously in those communities where modernism used to be strongest. It did take a measure of courage a couple of generations ago, before about 1880, to feel free to follow God's truth wherever it might lead, even though it might seem to undermine many cherished beliefs both about the Bible and the doctrines of the Christian faith. Many who showed such courage did not find it necessary to go to the extremes of modernism but that fact does not make the attitude of those who did any the less courageous. But, at least, in most places where there are Congregational churches, it has long ceased to require any courage to follow in that path. A combination of scientific humanism with a dash of idealism has long become the conventionally accepted background to the thought of most people even in the churches. What is radical and challenging in the world of today is 'the strange new world within the Bible' where God is real and acts, calling into question many of the deepest presuppositions of the culture which surrounds us and in which we share. Congregationalists, however, have been taught for so long that their central belief is one in freedom that they can feel free not to be troubled unduly by such ideas, since anything which is not immediately acceptable or which does not challenge them from within the accepted circle of ideas can be avoided as not being congruous with 'modern thought'. Too many sermons in Congregational churches today, therefore, sound like efforts on the part of ministers to take a text from Scripture, even when that appears to be necessary, and then to interpret it in such a way that all the sting and challenge is taken out of it and it is rendered innocuous and easily assimilable by the members of the congregation without requiring anything in the nature of a radical adjustment of outlook on their part. Paradoxically enough, one of the virtues of Congregational ministers, their persistent anxiety to make what they say clear and relevant to the needs of their congregations, has intensified this tendency. The result is that there is often only too much truth in the gibe that Congregationalism has now become the established church of the *petite bourgeoisie*, quickly shutting out any ideas or activity which disturb their complacency. A church which finds itself able to witness to spiritual freedom so easily and with such little internal agony should begin seriously to inquire whether it itself is not placing real freedom in jeopardy without realizing that it is doing so.

The danger of an emphasis on a wrong kind of freedom is underlined by the recent emergence of a political ideology which makes much of freedom and which claims a special affinity with Congregational church polity. This has received its most vigorous expression in Southern California, notably through the activities of the ebullient Dr. James Fifield of the First Congregational church of Los Angeles, but it is articulate in several other parts of America and has helped to form part of the opposition to the proposed merger of Congregational-Christian churches with the Evangelical and Reformed Church and to promote a singularly unscrupulous attack on the denomination's Council for Social Action. It has not received anything like the same clear expression in Britain, but there are enough indications that many older business men in British churches would probably find themselves in agreement with it. This ideology identifies Congregationalism with religious individualism, but its conception of individualism would be unconsciously deeply influenced not by the notion of every man thinking things out for himself and following the truth wherever it might lead, even if it led him into dangerous and unpopular ways, but by that of the nineteenth century archetypes of 'the rugged individualist' or the 'self-made man'. That is to say, it would have a pronounced economic character.

In fairness to the exponents of this point of view, it should be said that their belief in individualism would carry with it a strong emphasis on the importance of individual responsibility and of the duty of exercising justice and even charity in one's personal dealings. Without these, they probably would not feel that their individualism could claim to be considered 'religious'. At the same time, their witness on behalf of these is vitiated by their inability to recognize the fact that the relation between the individual and the community is one which constitutes a perennial problem to society and that the rights and responsibilities of both must be borne in mind. Congregationalism, indeed, has much to teach about the way in which this problem should be resolved. They also fail to see, either through naïvety or through the defect of vision caused by the corrupt influence of selfishness, that teaching about the impropriety of any restraint upon individual liberty nearly always serves the interest of the strong, especially the economically privileged, in a society like that of the present day. And they go on to fail to observe the implications of the fact that, for the most part, the economically privileged happen, by a curious chance, to be themselves. It is easy to blame business men for holding such crude and dangerous notions. Congregational ministers, however, do well to ask themselves whether their own confused teaching about the nature of freedom in relation to faith has not encouraged business men to believe that it is right to seek ecclesiastical sanction for the expression of their own self-interested prejudices.

Certainly, the Congregational witness on behalf of the freedom of the Spirit is needed today more than it ever was but, before it can carry conviction to their fellow-Christians, Congregationalists must first apply it firmly to themselves. Freedom is an empty word or a cloak for self-centredness if it is not founded freedom. Its foundation is in faith, and faith also is not an empty word but refers to a specific act of commitment to God as He has revealed Himself through Christ and made Himself known through the Spirit, the Spirit which guides the whole Church. The freedom which the Church knows is the reflection of the divine freedom and it is known only through obedience to the will of God, whose service is perfect freedom. That is the heart of Christianity and it is not peculiar to Congregationalism. What Congregationalists should have grasped more clearly than any other group of Christians, however, is that, if the Church is to remain an effective sphere for the operation of the freedom of God in His Spirit, that Church must always be mobile and supple, not so tied to secondary doctrinal and liturgical and institutional forms that it is never in a position to leave all and follow Christ. The

Church must always be prepared to die that it may live, to lose the whole world that it may gain its own soul. It was this insight which lay behind the classical Congregational insistence on the crown rights of the Redeemer in His Church. What Congregationalists have now to see is that when no prince or prelate or pope threatens their right to follow Christ, and when no hide-bound orthodoxy prevents them heeding any light and truth which God may cause to break forth from His Word, forces within their own life can be as enslaving as any outside pressure. 'The Congregational way of doing things' or 'the commonsense attitude of the people of our churches' or a superficial pride in alleged intellectual superiority or an isolationalist localism or a catch-penny topicality which is indifferent to the deeper meaning of Scripture and tradition can be as effective barriers to venturing into the unknown in the power of the Spirit as any more easily specified obstacles. Just as churches which call themselves Catholic have no automatic exemption from the perils of becoming false churches because they bear that mystic name, so Congregationalists cannot avoid being entangled again in the yoke of bondage from which Christ liberates us simply by trusting in the 'Congregational witness on behalf of freedom'. If we wish that witness in the present situation to be more than merely rhetorical, it must involve us in bold new acts of obedience to the will of God, which may mean death to some of our most cherished institutions and preconceptions. The bearing of this on the complex of questions discussed in the next section will quickly become clear.

V

The Local Church, the Ministry and the Great Church

There is no contradiction in the fact that Congregationalism emphasizes both freedom and fellowship, although there may appear to be on the surface. It is, perhaps, a happy accident that the alternative name for Congregationalism should be Independency. It prompts the outsider to inquire, 'How can people so independent form themselves into congregations, into bodies of people called out from their individualism into assembly?' Yet to the Congregationalist the words are not contradictory but complementary.[1] Because the local church is a gathering of Christ's people into the responsible fellowship of church order, it is answerable directly to Him for its life in that place and does not need to call on any outside body for the resources which are essential to maintain its life as the church in that place. Dr. Douglas Horton prefaces his book on Congregationalism[2] with a quotation from John Robinson which puts this very clearly:

'Now that the church, commonly called visible, is then most truly visible indeed, when it is assembled in one place,

[1] There is a well-known English Congregational theological college at Bradford which boasts the title, 'Yorkshire United Independent College'. On hearing that name for the first time, people frequently inquire how it manages to be both united and independent. The reason is that it represents a union of two old-established colleges of the Independent denomination in Yorkshire, but it is significant that no good Yorkshire Independent would notice anything incongruous in the designation.

[2] *Congregationalism: a Study in Church Polity* (Independent Press, London).

and the communion thereof, then most full, and entire, when all its members inspired, as it were, with the same presence of the Holy Ghost, do from the same pastor receive the same provocations of grace, at the same time and in the same place: when they all by the same voice "banding as it were together" (Tertul., Apol. Cap. 38) do with one accord pour out their prayers unto God: when they all participate of one, and the same holy bread (I. Cor. x, 17 . . .). This singular and sole assembly may, under Christ the head, use and enjoy every one of his institutions: the communion of saints combined together in solemn and sacred covenant, the Word of God, sacraments, censures and ministrations whatsoever by Christ appointed, and therewith, the same Christ's most gracious presence.'[1]

This passage holds fellowship and independence firmly together. The people of God are of one heart and one mind and the whole purpose of church order is to create and maintain their unity. Yet the Church as a body is unique of its kind and, possessing all the institutions of Christ, it possesses all that a church needs to sustain its being. It is independent, not in the sense of walking alone, but in the sense of being an indigenous and self-subsistent centre of Christian life. Possessing all the means of grace, no body on earth can be more fully the church than it, although many other similar bodies can be no less the church than it.

It should be carefully noted, however, that what constitutes a congregation as an independent church is not the fact that it gathers together but the fact that it possesses the ordinance of Christ for His Church. That is to say, it is the marks of Christ which are the marks of the Church, and not any generalized spirit of religious interest or any particular form of organization. Congregationalism takes very seriously the definition of classical Calvinism that wherever the Word is faithfully preached and the Sacraments administered

[1] John Robinson, *Works* (London, 1851), ii, 223; iii, 13, 15.

according to Christ's appointment, there the Church is to be found. It differs from other Reformed churches in this respect only in the extent to which it follows out the implications of this definition in relation to the local church's common life.

It would probably be true to say that, apart from some of their ministers, few Congregationalists would think readily of the Word and Sacraments as being constitutive of their church's existence or of their being closely related to the notion of Independency. They would be more naturally disposed, in these days, to think of the Spirit of Christ in this context and to relate their notion of Independency to His oft-quoted words, 'Where two or three are gathered together in my name, there am I in the midst.' It is important, therefore, to make clear that to give the primacy to the Word and Sacraments is not to say anything different from this but rather to say the same thing and to do so in a more developed and realistic way. For what is a church's ultimate source of assurance that it possesses Christ's Spirit? Is it that its members are good and kindly people and that they are diligent in the Lord's service? That should certainly be one of the marks of a Christian community but, for purposes of definition, it is a dubious and misleading criterion.[1] Churches, like individuals, manifest these qualities more clearly at some periods than at others and to lay all the emphasis upon them leads to Pharisaism and work-righteousness, while it obscures the fact that churches live, not from themselves, but from their Lord. Is it not more humble and reserved, and in the best sense more liberal, to say with Calvin that wherever the Word is preached and the Sacraments administered the Church is in some way present, since it is impossible that these should not bring forth some fruit? Or, to put it in

[1] See, for a trenchant discussion of this point, the pamphlet, *Congregationalism Today* (Independent Press, London, 1937), by Nathaniel Micklem.

language with which a modern Congregationalist might feel more readily at home, wherever Christ is preached and a determined and sincere effort made to ensure that it is His own teaching and not private ideas of individuals or groups about Him which is preached, and wherever people baptize in His name and meet together round His Table in His Spirit, the Church is in some sense present, however inadequate the life and organization of those people may be in many respects.

The chief hesitation which Congregationalists might have about that as a definition of the Church would probably be that it excludes the Society of Friends and the Salvation Army, two bodies which show clear evidence of being blessed by the Spirit of Christ. It is true that, however unpalatable the fact may be for many Christians, the witness of these bodies testifies to the fact that Christ is not tied to the specific form which the sacramental observances have possessed in the history of the Church. This is not the place to argue the whole of this complex matter, but that does not mean that Congregationalists may feel free to regard the Sacraments as merely optional. Quakerism may triumph over its lack of sacraments, but that does not necessarily contribute a virtue to Quakerism which other churches should emulate. It may indeed be largely responsible for the falsely 'spiritualizing' tendency and the complacent theological woolliness which so gravely impair the witness of modern Quakerism. And the Salvation Army, although it has shown signs of becoming a church in its own right, has always claimed to be an agency of the churches rather than a church in itself, a powerful weapon of evangelism and social service, but not always an admirable model of church order. In fact, it would be hard to find a form of church organization more remote from that which a Congregationalist would regard as ideal. The existence of such bodies as the Society of Friends and the Salvation Army certainly reminds us of the incompleteness and ambiguity of making even the presence of the Word and Sacraments constitutive marks of the visible Church, but they do not encourage us in the view that a more inclusive definition would not be even more misleading.

If it be granted that Independency does not mean atomistic individualism or secular democracy but that, through its possession of the Word and Sacraments, which are the means of grace, a church is able to take decisions for itself in freedom which are directly accountable to Christ, there remain serious questions which other churches would want to put to Congregationalism. What guarantee is there that the local church will preach the Word faithfully and that its Sacraments will be administered according to Christ's appointment? Is each congregation to be left as sole interpreter of the Word, calling whom they will to interpret it to them, according to their fancy of the moment, and leaving the field wide open for any man of easy manner and smooth tongue to prey upon the flock of Christ? Does not this principle lead straight to heresy? And not only to heresy but also to schism? For what effort is made in this system to ensure that the particular church will be of one heart and of one mind with the rest of Christ's body? Surely, there is a great overruling purpose of Christ for all His people and the Holy Spirit does not speak radically different words to different churches. There is such a thing as the mind of the whole Church. Congregationalism speaks much, in P. T. Forsyth's famous phrase, of the local church as the outcrop of the great Church. What procedure does Congregationalism adopt to ensure that its local churches are that and not merely haphazard collections of spiritually-minded individuals banded together simply for convenience's sake?

Congregationalists have to confess to members of other parts of the great Church that they have never faced these questions with quite the directness that they demand, nor tried to answer them with the thoroughness which they need. As we shall see, our associations and unions do provide a partial answer, and embedded in their procedure is an attitude which, as Dr. Douglas Horton claims,[1] has considerable importance for the way in which all churches should understand the nature and spirit of their communion with each other. Also it should be noted that many Congregational churches have formal Covenants, which are promulgated at the founding of a particular church and to which members are required to assent as they join the church. These are at pains to make clear the basis of that church's life and to leave no doubt in the minds either of other churches or of those who wish to join that particular church what manner of company they are joining. They are particular covenants which derive from the great Covenant God has made with His people in Jesus Christ and in that sense can be taken as a most explicit declaration of intention to be in communion with the great Church. An example of a modern church Covenant is printed as an appendix to this chapter. But even our Covenants do not answer completely this question and, as many Congregationalists clearly recognize today, we need to go to school to other churches to learn from them over these matters.

All the same, the consequences of this inadequacy have not been as serious as they might be because there is an institution within Congregationalism which does much of what these questioners require, even though its full significance in this respect has not always been clearly apprehended. The guarantee that a church is not led astray by false teaching and remains of one mind with the great Church is ultimately the same in Congregationalism as it is in other churches; it is the presence in the local church of the apostolic ministry.

Now this may sound very much like Episcopalianism and it is true that Episcopalians, and in particular Anglicans, fre-

[1] See *Congregationalism: A Study in Church Polity*, pp. 85–90.

quently put their point of view in this way. But they must bear a heavy responsibility for the continued division and confusion of the non-Roman churches of the West because they so frequently make the point in an unduly limited and formal way, so that it is hard to grasp the substance of what they are trying to express. Partly for polemical reasons in seeking to justify their continued separation from non-Anglican Protestant churches, they have defined possession of the apostolic ministry almost exclusively in terms of the regularity of external commissioning, so that a church could be recognized as a church by inquiring whether it possessed a ministry empowered, both legally and sacramentally, to perform its office by other ministers standing in what is claimed to be an unbroken chain of succession from the apostles. Congregationalists, while not denying the value of such a succession if circumstances have permitted its maintenance, would deny that its possession gave any kind of binding guarantee of the authenticity of a church. In so far as such guarantees are possible, and it should be remembered always that at best they are so only relatively, they are more reliably provided by the preaching of the Word in Scripture and the celebration of the Sacraments with the intention of fulfilling Christ's ordinance. The guarantee of the authenticity of the Word and the Sacraments themselves, which in the nature of the case is an even less palpable matter, is provided more realistically by the nature of the ministry[1] which dispenses them than by any automatic invocation of historical succession which, as 'the question of Anglican orders' in relation to Rome itself makes clear, is a fruitful source of disputes and efforts at self-justification. Given the broken and confused order which all churches possess under modern conditions, the most practical step a church can take to ensure that when it

[1] This is not the same point as that relating to the moral character of the ministry mentioned in the Thirty-nine Articles.

tries to obey God's Word in Scripture it does so in the context of the whole experience of the great Church and that when it admits children to baptism and sits in fellowship around the Lord's Table it does so as part of the great family of God's people, is to ensure that it possesses a minister who is trained and experienced in the ways of the great Church.

After all, what is the minister supposed to do in a Congregational church or, for that matter, in any other Reformed church? He is not simply a president of the assembly nor yet a clerk, who reads and speaks on behalf of the congregation what anyone else of ordinary competence is equally capable of reading and speaking. He is a member of the church specially called and gifted and trained to enable the local church to look at itself and its vocation in the setting of the whole purpose of God for all His people. Episcopalians quite rightly insist that the bishop is the representative in the local church of the great Church, but Congregationalists would want to say that he is this not simply because he is commissioned to act as such by a corporation of bishops who represent the whole, however desirable such commissioning may be, but because of the function he performs in relation to the Word and the Sacraments. It is these which most effectively represent the great Church in the local church, it is these which are its primary marks of catholicity, because they represent the universal Christ who is Lord of all and who brings all His people with Him wherever He goes. The Bible which is preached is not the possession of one particular church. It is the possession of all the churches and a great body of thought and knowledge and fruitful spiritual experience has gathered round it in the course of the ages. When a particular church gathers round the Bible on the Lord's Day to hear what God is speaking to it from His Word it will lose touch with the Spirit of God and mis-hear the Word if it steps out of the context of this rich experience, which is, of course, not only experience of the Bible itself but also of what God has said and done to His people throughout history and what He is doing now in His dealings with them at the present time. It is the purpose of the minister to do this on behalf of the Church. He represents the mind of the great Church in the local church and does so not merely formally or symbolically, but concretely, in his preaching, in his planning and conduct of the worship and in the guidance and advice he proffers in church meeting and in personal counsel. If it possesses a faithful ministry, the local church is able to think and discern the spirits and pray and praise and order its affairs, not as an isolated unit doing that which is right in its own eyes, but as a responsible part of the great Church. Although all ministries must be defective both in authority and insight while the great Church remains divided, yet it is possible for a ministry to guide a church in responsible conformity to the Spirit even in the midst of division. It can be the instrument of that interior ecumenicity of which we spoke in the first chapter.

When the idea is put in this way, it may strike some Congregationalists as novel, but it is, in fact, an idea which is implicit in the way Congregationalism has always thought of the ministry. This is proved by the great emphasis which classic Congregationalism laid on the maintenance of a 'learned' ministry. Whatever may be said of some of their children, the Congregationalist fathers would certainly not have taken this to refer solely to the desirability of having ministers who could produce highly polished sermons, nicely garnished with literary references, for the delectation of their admirers. They meant learned in the Scriptures and in the ways of God with His people and in the wisdom of the Church throughout the ages. The end of such learning was to bring the understanding of the will of God in a particular church into line with that of the great Church, so that it could justify its title to independence by manifesting a judgment as responsible and as informed as any other part of the Church.

This is not to suggest that the possession of a 'learned ministry' is a sufficient link between the local church and the great Church. Congregationalism's need to strengthen other links which exist will be considered later in this chapter. But the importance and effectiveness of this link which already exists are often overlooked. With a learned ministry, Congregationalism may not possess a church polity which is in every respect ideal but it is delivered from the excesses of spiritual anarchy. That ministry may itself be defective in important particulars, both in the extent of the recognition it receives from other branches of the great Church and in the ways in which it is able to exercise its own responsibility to other particular churches than its own within its own denomination, but, if it is a ministry which seeks to present Christ as the Scriptures declare Him and which seeks to enter into communion with all who have known Him, the possibility of arriving at genuine ecumenicity is always open in a Congregational church.

This emphasis on the importance of the ministry as the ecumenical link in Congregationalism is not meant to imply a clericalist view of our polity. The centre of decision in a Congregational church remains the church meeting. The function of the ministry is to help the church meeting ensure that its decisions are taken with full responsibility. It is the Word and Sacraments which constitute the church, not the ministry, even though the aid of the learned ministry is necessary for their proper maintenance. Congregationalists can contemplate the possibility of the Word sometimes being preached and the Sacraments administered by someone who is not ordained to lifelong service in the office of ministry. This should happen only in special circumstances and should be accompanied by a recognition that their responsible administration might be seriously weakened unless supervised by a learned ministry, but it, at least, indicates that ministry is a special function in the church and that the church is not irrevocably tied to one highly stylized form of it. The notion that nothing should ever be done in a Congregational church except through the minister is a dangerous one just as much as in the secularized form of it, which has such currency in these days, that the minister is to be regarded as the 'spiritual leader' of the congregation, around whose personality, whether in the pulpit or as an organizer, all its activities are built up. The healthiest churches are those where, on the local level, leadership comes from the diaconate rather than from the ministry. This, in fact, frequently happens. Ministers tend to move from one church to another after a number of years and have many interests outside the local church but the deacons remain and they often know their own church and its locality as their minister does not.[1] On the national and international level, as we shall see, the situation may well be different, but in the local church ministers should strive carefully to limit the opportunities presented to them for exercising secular power. They are there to inspire, guide, and instruct their deacons and church members, but they do well to keep themselves in the background. The decline of the Victorian cult of the popular preacher, although it partly represents a falling off in the public authority of the pulpit, has brought substantial compensations with it. The City Temple of Joseph Parker's day may have fulfilled many valuable functions, but it is hard to think of an institution less

[1] Deacons in Congregational churches perform functions similar to those performed by elders in Presbyterian churches. They are not part of the professional ministry but are elected from the church meeting to share with the minister in the administration, oversight and guidance of the congregation. An average-size Congregational church in England would be likely to have twelve deacons. It would be quite usual for two or three of these to be women.

like a true Congregational church. Church life is the common life of a family of Christian people. It is built around Christ, who meets with His people in Word and Sacraments. These need the learned ministry for their effective administration. But it is the most complete betrayal of his function for a minister to deflect attention from Christ, whose servant he is, to himself.

The local church expresses the life of the great Church in a particular place through the presence within it of the universal Word and Sacraments and a ministry trained to administer them in an ecumenical way. But how does the local church give expression to its concrete wider responsibilities? What means does it possess for participating directly in the life of the great Church? Here, even when the best has been said for it, Congregationalism is at its weakest. T. W. Manson's friendly criticisms of Bernard Manning and of R. W. Dale in his *The Church's Ministry* are undoubtedly apposite, and Congregationalists, as they themselves very freely recognize today, need to add, as Manson suggests, a sixth Congregational Principle to Dale's five, 'By the will of Christ every Christian church has an obligation to care for and be in fellowship with other Christian churches.'[1] And they need not only to acknowledge that principle, which is, after all, inherent in their own tradition, but to create more adequate organs than they now possess for putting it into effect.

First, a Congregational church will have to recognize that, even in its own locality, it is unlikely to be in a position to claim to be the whole Christian community. Few Congregationalists would now wish to assert that theirs alone is the true church but not all are prepared to accept its corollary, that they have an obligation to seek full fellowship with their neighbours who are gathered together into church order under different denominations. This full fellowship does not mean

[1] *The Church's Ministry* (Hodder and Stoughton, London, 1948), p. 94.

merely fraternal co-operation in joint projects and occasional visits. These may be necessary steps towards full fellowship but they are far from reaching it. Congregationalism, on its own principles, should lay the greatest stress on seeking to draw near into unity with other churches at the local level. A church which retreats into self-satisfied isolation from other churches in its own locality in the name of Independency shows only that it has not begun to understand what Independency means. How local churches can draw together in this way is a large and complicated question which must be answered differently in different situations. What must be clear is that it is not an optional enthusiasm for the ecumenical movement but the nature of Congregationalism itself which lays this necessity upon Congregational churches to draw nearer to other churches in their own neighbourhood.

Secondly, it has, of course, always been recognized in Congregationalism that the local church is not the only form of the church. 'The communion of the churches with each other' quickly became a matter for discussion among Independents and amidst all the changes and confusion of the seventeenth century councils and synods were formed and even in the period of the relative decline of churchmanship in the eighteenth century many of the county associations in England received their birth. The Congregational Union of England and Wales was not founded till 1831, but that may have been partly due to the difficulties involved in forming a substantial national body earlier, and the London Missionary Society was formed nearly forty years before. In New England the situation was different because of the connection with the state, whose approval had to be received before a church could be founded for many generations, but the development of councils was both earlier and more vigorous than in England. The popular notion among Catholics that Protestants in general and Congregationalists in particular believe only in an invisible church, which becomes visible only in local congregations, is erroneous. Protestants have a different conception from many Catholics of how the Church becomes visible, a conception which faces the implications of the Ascension of our Lord and of the freedom of access to Him which is now possible to all men through the Spirit, but they would insist as strongly as Catholics that visibility is an obvious characteristic of the Church in its earthly existence. As we have already seen, it is their insistence upon this which led Congregationalists to lay such emphasis on the importance of the local church, as being the Church in its most immediate and palpable and inescapable form. What has been at fault in Congregationalism has been not so much its conception of visibility as its conception of locality. It has always recognized the need for a communion of churches with each other but it has not always seen clearly how much of the real life of individual churches should flow through that communion and it has often had too limited a conception of what a local church should be. There is, for example, a case for saying that under present conditions of life a nation provides a genuine locale and that a national council of churches should consider how it can express some of the characteristics of a local church as well as how it can exercise powers granted to it by local churches in the more restricted sense.

The General Council of the Congregational-Christian Churches of America is more fortunate in this respect, although it, too, has its problems, but the Congregational Union of England and Wales has had occasion to do a great deal of heart-searching about its relation to individual churches and to county unions in recent years. The matters involved are complex and still require much further clarification before any proposals for reform can be pressed, but certain points of principle may, by now, be held to be fairly clear.

First, the motive behind the formulation of Congregationalist polity is to ensure that the responsibility of the Church to its Lord should be localized and defined as precisely as possible. It is not to ensure that each individual congregation should continue in the possession of the maximum amount of freedom of action at all costs. If it seems good to the members of local churches that they require an organ of communion with each other which will the more effectively be the instrument of God's common purpose for them, it is their duty to ensure that it is a responsible instrument. It must have the power to follow the bidding of the Church's Lord wherever it may lead and to call the local churches to join with it in the ways appropriate to their varying circumstances. Otherwise, the crown rights of the Redeemer in His Church, the spiritual freedom of Christ's body, will be imperilled by the dictatorial pressure of local churches themselves. A body which has responsibility before God for large parts of the life of His Church which it cannot fulfil because it has power only to recommend and not to act, unless it does so surreptitiously, is in an intolerable position from the point of view of the fundamental intention of Congregational polity itself. It is not merely permissible but essential that an organ of the communion of the churches with each other, which in the nature of the case becomes a form of the Church, should receive the powers necessary for the effective fulfilment of its function.

Secondly, it does not follow from this that because some ecclesiastical powers should reside in the wider fellowship of churches all should do so. Thorough-going Presbyterianism is not the only alternative to atomistic Congregational autonomy. It is both right and possible to give certain powers to a Council, which the local church, acting in freedom, recognizes as a more responsible body to receive such powers than itself, while it retains other powers firmly in its own hands. Action of this kind, under the conditions of modern life where, even in Congregationalism, the pressure towards centralization is so intense, will serve indeed to limit as well as to make more effective the use of powers which councils possess. At present, it often happens that while the fiction is maintained that a union or association has no power beyond those of recommendation, in practice the realities of the situation give it a great deal of power which, because it is unrecognized, is also not checked. Only the sense of responsibility with which officers of unions and associations exercise their powers makes this situation much less dangerous than it might easily become.

Congregationalists frequently insist today that their councils should be given more authority but generally go on to explain that, of course, this authority should be exercised in a ministerial rather than a legal way. Certainly all authority in the church should be exercised in a ministerial way but it is hard to resist the suspicion that this phrase is used to cover up a reluctance to face the fact that this authority, if it is to be real, will need to have a legal side. This is a part of the long-standing distrust among Congregationalists of anything in the nature of ecclesiastical law, which is the more interesting because so many lawyers happen to be Congregationalists. This distrust of law in the church is partly a well-founded distrust of legalism and of the clerical rigorism which too easily creeps into so conservative an institution as the church. It is undoubtedly the case that churches should strive to reach a common mind or agree to differ in charity rather than appeal to courts, and their institutional life should not be so organized as to encourage such appeals. Yet it is a dangerous fallacy to suppose that a church can dispense with law altogether, any more than, in a sinful world, it can dispense with discipline. There can be little doubt that some, at least, of the reluctance of Congregationalists to give specific and defined powers to councils which would be binding on local churches is due to an uneasy feeling that it would commit local churches to taking both councils and themselves more seriously and responsibly than they would find comfortable.

The whole matter of what functions are properly performed by councils and what by the local church is clearly one of great complexity which must occupy the attention of Congregationalists in the near future much more than it has yet done. A few things are already sufficiently clear, however, if only because they are already done by existing unions in an informal way. The terms of the communion of the churches with each other obviously have to be defined by churches meeting together in council. There must be agreement as to what constitutes a Congregational church and whether any particular church shall be admitted to its communion. There is, in fact, an agreement on this subject but it must be re-examined and put on a more responsible basis. And what is true of churches is also true of ministers. There must be agreement as to what constitutes a Congregational minister and as to who is to be admitted to or expelled from the Congregational ministry. The council clearly has a right to have a say in who shall or shall not be a Congregational minister and also in the matter of where ministers should be placed. Once again, this is informally recognized but it needs to be placed on a much more responsible basis, at least in England. In this respect, where the association ordains, America is in advance of England. There must be provision for the general oversight of ministers. We have seen how much depends in Congregationalism on the ministry. If a minister misleads a church it is peculiarly hard, under the Congregational system, for a church to remain in communion of heart and mind with the rest of the great Church. The wider fellowship has an interest, therefore, in ensuring that a minister is being broadly faithful to his charge. And if there have to be courts of ministerial discipline there must also be courts where disputes and scandals within churches or between churches can be settled. These questions bristle with difficulties and produce visions in the minds of Congregationalists of things they most hate, heresy trials and church lawyers and petty ecclesiastical intrigues. But the way to avoid these real dangers is not by pretending that we need not face the problems which other, more fully organized churches have to face, but by striving to create a machinery to deal with them which expresses the best of our tradition of respect for liberty of conscience and of empiricism. Apart from anything else, as the question of reunion with other churches, especially those of Presbyterian character, becomes more and more relevant it will be increasingly difficult for us to avoid making up our minds on these issues.

There can be no doubt, either, that under the conditions of modern life the scope of the work of our councils will have greatly to be extended. This again involves painful problems, which have as yet been faced only in the most tentative way. Many aspects of the life of churches today can be dealt with only on the national and international levels. While it is still probably true that the most effective forms of church extension are those promoted by local churches, the scale and complexity of the operations involved and the mobility of populations make it imperative that great powers be placed into the hands of councils in these matters. Also, many forms of evangelism and Christian obedience, in political and industrial and cultural life, cannot be effectively organized from the local church. In order that local churches themselves should obtain adequate Christian guidance on many of the affairs of the day and should express their care for each other, large-scale intelligence and service organizations are needed which must be supported by all the churches. Quite apart from that, there is the need for an ever-growing class of chaplains and specialist church workers in all the institutions of the modern world, from mental hospitals to armies, which are not organized on a local basis. The churches have successfully adapted their own work to cope with many of these changes and it is merciful that it has been found possible to do much of the pioneering work on an inter-denominational basis. But work of this kind is for ever growing and it is doubtful whether churches in general and Congregational churches in particular have yet adjusted their minds, their organization and their finances to the new pattern of church life which is emerging. The church is being forced by the conditions of the time to be an army on the march again. Too many Congregational churches act as though they were still besieged cities, sending out only occasional forays into the country around them.

This will inevitably mean a strengthening of the central organization of Congregationalism. But there is good reason to hope that it will also mean a widespread recognition of the limitations and inadequacy of Congregationalism even at its most effective. The more Congregationalism faces the challenges and opportunities of the great Church in these days the more realistically will it have to acknowledge that, like all denominations, whether they give themselves the title 'Catholic' or not, it is but one part of the whole Church and can only speak as one voice among many. It cannot pretend, however strong its organization may become, to be the whole Body or to say to any other part of the Body, 'I have no need of you'. This does not mean that Congregationalism cannot function responsibly to God in its distinctive councils, nor strive to act in its own domestic affairs as a faithful member of the whole. Obviously, it is the main theme of this book that it can and should. But it also means some voluntary surrender of sovereignty on the part of Congregationalism and its councils to other and more widely representative bodies which also possess a conciliar character. This will not be turning away from our own heritage but its fulfilment in a more complete and more all-embracing fellowship than was ever possible to our fathers.

COVENANT OF THE CONGREGATIONAL CHURCH ESTABLISHED AT BANSTEAD, SURREY, 1946

We, acknowledging God to be our God and Jesus Christ His Son to be our Lord and the Holy Spirit to be our Guide, commit ourselves to one another to live together in church order as a company of Christ's people.

We seek to fulfil the will of God, as declared in Scripture, in bearing one another's burdens and sharing each other's joys, in welcoming the stranger and befriending the poor and lonely, in caring for the young and building up our families as part of the great family of God.

We promise to endeavour by prayer, personal service, and conscientious giving to proclaim the Kingdom of God at home and abroad, and to fulfil His will in all human relationships in which we have part, whether social, economic, or international.

We intend that our Church should be in communion with the churches of the Congregational order, but seek by God's grace, fellowship with other churches, especially those of our neighbourhood, working and praying together with them for the unity of Christ's Church in the world.

Finally, we commend ourselves to the whole Church of Christ on earth, and commit ourselves to the Word of God our Father, in the knowledge that He will not leave us nor forsake us, and that at the last all will be gathered together in Christ our Redeemer.

This covenant is acknowledged by all members on joining the church. It was originally drafted by a minister but was considerably altered in detail by the members of the church before it was finally agreed upon.

VI

Worship and the Common Life

It has long been the custom for Congregationalists to assure each other that all is not well with Congregationalism in regard to its public worship. Certainly, there is evidence to prove that their dissatisfaction is well-grounded and that there is room for reform. Much of this chapter will be taken up with suggestions for reform, along lines indicated both by participation in the ecumenical movement and by a fresh understanding of our own best traditions. Yet it is well to remind ourselves and others that the same considerations which prompt our desire for reform also remind us that there are many virtues in our practice of public worship which we often take for granted and which may be of help to other churches.

In contrast to churches with a fixed liturgy, Congregationalism has always been disposed to emphasize the free and active movement of the Spirit in worship, valuing sincerity and spontaneity of expression more than the due performance of a rite. It cannot always claim to have understood the right relation between the free movement of the Spirit and fixed forms, although it sometimes has, and it has often had a naïve conception of what constitutes sincerity and spontaneity. This has exposed it to grave dangers, but it has also enabled it to bring out the value of some sides of worship which many other churches have neglected. If it has not always been clear about the precise relation between the Real Presence of Christ and the sacramental elements, it has often shown a clearer sense of the Real Presence of Christ in the Spirit as a living, guiding power in the whole congregation than many bodies which have most strongly affirmed belief in the Real Presence of Christ.

This is part of the reason why the sermon flourishes as an institution in Congregational churches. They are not unique among Reformed churches in this respect, of course, but it is probably true to say that the amount of time and thought given to the preparation of sermons is as high in Congregational churches as in any other and the amount of pains taken to ensure that congregations follow and understand them probably greater. It is true that, partly because of this desire that there should be effective communication between preacher and congregation, the sermon has frequently become trivialized in modern times, yet at least it can be said that an appeal can be made to our own best traditions more clearly and readily than to any other court in seeking to reform this situation. That church is indeed unfortunately placed where no stirring of expectancy can be detected when the people settle down to hear the sermon, which indicates that the true notion of what a sermon should do has not been entirely lost from our midst. The training and preparation of most Congregational ministers today are such that, in England at least, they have chiefly themselves to blame if they do not understand what constitutes faithful preaching and if they find themselves ill-equipped to do it.

Related to this is the comparatively high standard of discrimination in choice of hymns frequently to be found in Congregational churches, at least as far as England is concerned. The position is, perhaps, not quite so happy in America. It may be claiming too much to say, as Bernard Manning and others have, that, like the Methodists, our hymn-books are our liturgy. Such a remark itself displays a misleading conception of the nature of liturgy and probably exaggerates the influence that hymns can have. But Congregationalists do participate more directly in the service through their hymns than in any other way and share more active interest in and understanding of them than almost any other church except the Methodist. The new hymn-book of English Congregationalists, *Congregational Praise* may justly claim to be one of the very best hymn-books designed for popular use in the English tongue and compares very favourably indeed with hymn-books used in churches of more Catholic type. The church of Isaac Watts still maintains its tradition of contributing richly to the praises of Zion.

A third virtue of our worship is that it is closely related to the corporate life of the church as a Christian community. Here again, we fall far short of our ideal but the ideal has never been lost sight of and has often been effectively realized. In the absence of a book of common prayer, the conduct of our services appears to be too much at the mercy of the personal inclinations of the minister. Yet there are important safeguards against mere eccentricity in this matter which are often overlooked. Not only is the minister supposed to be a 'learned' minister in the sense discussed in the last chapter but also he is considered to be the representative of the congregation whom he leads and with whom he is expected to stand in an intimate pastoral relationship. The prayer of the minister in leading the congregation is meant to be, in a specific way, a prayer arising out of the family life of the church and closely connected with its needs. The old notion among the Independents, as among many other churches of similar type, was that a special 'gift' was required for public prayer, as for preaching, in contrast to the attitude of the Established Church, which appeared to require only the clerkly ability to be able to read the Book of Common Prayer. Whether that is fair to the Prayer Book is an open question, but the notion of the gift of prayer called attention to an aspect of the life of worship which is often neglected by the highly formalized churches. They may present a very much tidier picture of themselves to the casual visitor than do most Congregational churches which, like other Free Churches, put on a very second-rate pageant. But if that casual visitor stays and shares in the life of a Congregational church for a long period, he is likely to find that its worship may have more reality and depth than were first apparent, because it arises out of and seeks to guide the common life of the congregation. Like the American nation they did so much to form, Congregational churches lack the gift of putting their best face before the world.

Yet, when all has been said, the widespread dissatisfaction with the character of our public worship which is felt by Congregationalists of more than one school of thought has much justification, and there are few places where we can learn more readily from the experience of other parts of the Church. At the same time, it is obviously important that we learn with discrimination and with a clear grasp of first principles. Part of our trouble in the recent past has been that, in our desire to achieve more 'worshipful' services, we have borrowed without discrimination from Anglicanism. The influence on Congregationalism of Anglican Gothic architecture and the disposition of the church interior which goes with it has, on the whole, been baneful. That influence is still intense in America where, it has been ruefully observed, the majority of churches being built today in the old Colonial New England style are put up by the Roman Catholics. The regrettable consequences of modelling the main Sunday service in a Congregational church on the modified choir office of Matins instead of upon the Holy Communion have frequently been pointed out by Congregational scholars in recent years.

The primary need of Congregationalism in relation to worship today, therefore, is not to copy this or that form or procedure from other churches, although it may often be desirable to do so. It is to understand anew the doctrine of the Church in its fullness and from that to derive a clear conception of what Dom Gregory Dix has taught us to call 'the shape of the liturgy'. It is to understand how the parts of the Church's worship are related to each other and how what happens in worship is related, in its turn, to the rest of the life of the Church as a whole. This conception of the shape of the liturgy was present in classical Reformed teaching, as the liturgies of the churches of the Reformation indicate, but even there it was not always as clearly articulated as many other parts of Christian doctrine, and in the eighteenth and early nineteenth centuries it was often lost sight of, with the result that the operative tradition of many Congregational churches is extremely vague on many of these matters.

All the same, the main lines of our essential position in regard to worship and the common life can be traced without serious difficulty. In practice, even though, as we have seen, they would not all be readily at home with this form of words, most Congregationalists would accept the dictum of Calvin that it is the Word and Sacraments which constitute the Church as the Church. They do this because they are Christ's appointed means of grace, by which He maintains living communion with His people. The Church's life is, therefore, built around them. The main purpose of worship is to hear God's Word in Jesus Christ, declared in the Scriptures and related to the particular needs of that congregation in the setting of the experience of the whole Church, and to realize Christ's living presence in the sacrament of His body and blood. We have seen that Congregationalism's witness to the importance of God's Word in the preaching is not inadequate. It is not so clear that it gives their full value to the Sacraments of the Lord's Supper and Baptism. While it can be argued that there are some communions which so exalt the Sacraments as to lose the proportion of faith, the sacramental life of most

Congregational churches is undoubtedly weak as compared with that of large tracts of Christendom. That is not to say that a rich interpretation of the Sacraments is not to be found in Congregational history and among modern theologians nor that they are commonly regarded lightly in modern Congregational churches. Anglo-Catholic writers, avid for atrocity stories, have made far too much of the notion that Congregationalists regard Baptism as optional. A few do, and the laxity of Congregational discipline allows them to practise such an attitude, but they can claim little authority in Congregational teaching for such a position and the overwhelming majority of Congregationalists are baptized and cherish their Baptism. And, although Congregational attitudes and procedures at the Lord's Supper may sometimes leave much to be desired from the point of view of other churches, the Lord's Supper is regularly celebrated in Congregational churches and is usually a more genuinely corporate act of the congregation than it is in churches where celebrations are more frequent. Yet, as many modern Congregationalists recognize, it is in their sacramental life that they have most to learn from other churches. That they are learning, and learning fast, while retaining and developing the Reformed insistence on the close relation between Word and Sacrament, is a hopeful sign.

They are, however, in a better position than some other churches to grasp a neglected truth about the worship of the church, its close relation to the church's common life. For a church which has the most impeccable preaching and sacramental administration and lacks organs of expression of its common life which strive to be responsible to Christ its Head is in danger of becoming a mere façade. This danger Congregationalism tries to overcome by its institution of the church meeting.

There has been a widespread revival of interest in the place of the congregation in the life of the church in these days, some of it in unexpected places. An active movement exists in the Church of England for the organization of parish meetings and for the development of a strong family feeling among the church members of each parish.[1] Even in the Roman Catholic church, notably in France, a very lively and original concern has developed to integrate the congregation into the church's life and not to make it the mere appendage of the hierarchy. This is a situation which should give much encouragement to Congregationalists and provides them with their chief ecumenical opportunity, but they are often unable to make the most of it because they themselves do not always see how the church meeting fits into the structure not merely of the church's social life but also of its worship. Congregationalists themselves have often tended to think of the church meeting chiefly as a meeting for business, where members might have their say in regard to the general conduct of the affairs of their own church, on the analogy of secular democracy, and have not seen the point which those who have approached it from the background of churches of very different type have clearly grasped, that it is a part of church order, leading out from the preaching of the Word and the celebration of the Sacraments and controlled in its procedure by the nature of the spiritual realities with which it has to deal.

There are at least four ways in which the church meeting can be seen to be different from any other kind of meeting. In the first place, it makes a conscious effort to be ruled by the Spirit of Jesus Christ. This is where its connection with the Word and the Sacraments becomes most manifest. The minister of the Word and Sacraments should preside over the church meeting as he does in public worship and there are analogies between his functions in both places. The kind of equipment needed for the service of the Word and Sacraments is also the kind of equipment needed for presiding over

[1] News of its activities is given in its magazine, *Parish and People.*

the church meeting. The minister, as we have seen, is the representative of the great Church in the local church and this receives very concrete expression in the church meeting. When the local church is gathered together to deliberate how it should obey God in its own place, it needs the help of one who is equipped to interpret to it the mind of the great Church as it affects the issues under discussion, one who brings with him the witness of 'tradition' in the widest sense into the life of the local church. Over many matters in the church meeting, the minister has no more right to speak than any other member and he should be scrupulous to avoid speaking whenever possible. But over many others, and they the weightier, he is in the midst to call the attention of the assembled company to the teaching of Scripture and the experience of the Church throughout the ages and the practice of other churches in relation to matters similar to those with which that particular church is now dealing, so that as the church waits, in prayer and discussion, upon the Spirit, it may strive to ensure that its mind is sufficiently open to all that the Spirit may say. The church meeting is the most obvious place where a particular church tries to express that interior ecumenicity of which we spoke in the last chapter.

Secondly, it is not a place where people are free casually to blow in and let off steam about anything to do with the life of the church which may be exercising them at the moment. It presupposes a responsible discipline of understanding of the ways of God with His people and of how His people should conduct themselves in transacting His business. Where an educated membership of this kind does not exist, a church meeting should be prepared to give a good deal of authority to its appointed leaders or else submit to a voluntary limitation of its authority in some directions in favour of an organ of the wider fellowship such as a County Union. An educated membership here, of course, does not necessarily mean a membership possessing a high standard of secular education. It means educated in the same sense as the ministry should be 'learned', educated in the ways of God with His people. Many of the wisest and most experienced leaders of particular churches are people who have had little formal schooling. The point is that no church meeting can dare to say of any of its decisions, 'It seemed good to the Holy Spirit and to us' unless those who have taken that decision have learnt how to discern the mind of the Spirit by constant and intelligent attendance on the means of grace and participation in the affairs of the church meeting.

Thirdly, the church meeting differs on important points of procedure from most forms of secular democracy, whether direct or representative, except in so far as they have themselves, as in England, come under the influence of ecclesiastical procedures. Its purpose is not to gratify the wishes of a majority of its members; it is to discern the will of God. And since that will is one will, that means that a deliberate effort must be made by the church meeting to reach a common mind, with the rule that the effort must become the more determined in proportion to the importance of the matter under discussion. Members meet together in order to seek each other's help in discerning God's will and that search is frustrated if they concentrate on scoring debating points off each other or on trying to override each other. Where division arises, each must listen anxiously to the other, putting the most positive interpretation on what he says, lest the Spirit be speaking through him. And this holds even if the dissentient be in a minority of one. This is a very important point to bear in mind when the minister may disagree with the rest of the church meeting over a matter where he can claim the support of Scripture and the mind of the great Church for his judgment. In such a situation, the church meeting would be well advised to seek, in the friendliest way, the help of a representative of the wider fellowship of churches. Over a secondary or merely technical matter, a church meeting may sometimes resort to the rough expedient of a vote. Questions like whether the church boiler should be lit on Saturday evening or early on Sunday morning, which are apt to take up an undue amount of time, can reasonably be settled by a quick vote, lest the complicated procedure of striving to reach a common mind over such matters might divert the church's attention from more serious affairs. But over matters of spiritual moment voting should be resorted to only when the effort to reach a common mind has failed, and with a recognition of the spiritual weakness which has produced such failure. The characteristic procedure of the church meeting is to reach unity in the Spirit, in the knowledge that Christ is not divided.

Fourthly, the church meeting should frankly recognize the limits of its own competence. It should be prepared to accept the fact that many of the affairs of the church are best dealt with in relative privacy by minister and deacons, whose authority it should define and safeguard. This is obviously true of many matters of discipline of individuals. It should not be greedy for arbitrary and unlimited power, after the manner of many truculent church meetings of the nineteenth century, especially in the North of England, and refuse to give authority to exercise their function to its own officers or to submit to the guidance of organs of the wider fellowship in matters over which it has no obvious competence. Notably, it should recognize that while it might reasonably have the chief voice in choosing its own minister, it is not necessarily right that it should have the only voice but that the wider fellowship is also entitled to be heard. And when the church meeting fails and becomes divided, it should have the humility to submit itself to the judgment of the wider fellowship and to abide by its findings.

It can hardly be claimed that there are many church meetings which have this clear understanding of their nature and worthily display all these characteristics. Yet, in England at least, there are few Congregational churches in which the church meeting does not function with a fair measure of effectiveness as an essential organ of the church's life. That is as well, for without instructed and responsible church meetings Congregationalism rapidly becomes one of the worst forms of church order and wastes the most precious gift which it holds in trust for the whole Church.

It is important, therefore, that Congregationalism should recapture its understanding of the inner coherence of its own forms of worship and common life and that it should make the best of its own heritage. Without these it cannot make its own contribution to the ecumenical movement. But it needs equally to modify and develop its forms of worship and common life in such a way that it draws nearer in fellowship to the rest of Christendom. The worship of a typical Congregational church, as we have seen, may be very well adjusted to the needs of a particular congregation as that congregation conceives them but it may make it excessively hard for the newcomer or even for the congregation itself to have the sense of worshipping with the whole Church. It is this, as much as any eccentricities of dogma, which serves to make Congregationalism sectarian in outlook. There are three ways, increasingly followed in modern Congregationalism, by which this danger may be overcome.

The first is to redefine the relation between so-called free prayer and set forms of prayer in such a way that they complement and do not contradict each other. The freedom which free prayer possesses is that of the Spirit. The Spirit is not the particular spirit of an individual, who may be whimsical or eloquent or prosy or insensitive, but the Spirit of the Word. The Spirit which moves the heart of the minister in prayer is also moving the heart of his congregation and it is also the Spirit of Jesus Christ, who inspires the Scriptures and who has sustained the Church in its worship throughout the ages. This Spirit may very well prompt the minister to pray quite spontaneously as he leads his people in prayer on the Lord's Day but if it does it is likely to do so in such a way that the congregation quickly recognizes its appropriateness and is able to follow without any loss of unity in prayer. And since public prayer is common prayer, set against the background not only of the life of the particular congregation but also of the whole Church, it can be confidently asserted that such moments of spontaneity should be the exception rather than the rule. Nothing is more unseemly and artificial, as the experience of many denominations proves, than a cult of spontaneity in worship, and nothing degenerates more quickly into a stereotyped form, which is the more lifeless because it is only what is left when real spontaneity has departed. Congregationalists, as they increasingly do and as some of them always have, should frankly recognize the spiritual value of set prayers, whether in the form of prayers prepared beforehand by a learned and gifted minister, who draws upon the experience in prayer of the Church throughout the ages, or in the form of a printed liturgy, which is accepted by many churches and familiar to their members. The Spirit does not require us to offer freshly minted words when we approach the throne of grace every Sunday morning and it is an exercise of proper piety and humility to use forms familiar to long generations of believers and truly sanctified by usage. To reject such prayer is to exaggerate the extent of the area in which genuine freedom is either possible or desirable. It is a matter of great spiritual importance to insist that there must always be a place for free prayer in the service but it is likely to be more authentically free if it arises out of a background of set prayer than if it operates in a void. In fact, what measure of coherence so-called free prayer in the Protestant tradition has possessed in the past has been largely due to the way in which it moved always within the setting of Biblical images and quotations which were familiar and luminous for both minister and people. In striking a proper balance between free and set prayer, Congregational churches, like many others, have much to learn from the modern practice of the Church of England, which has revitalized the Prayer Book to a remarkable degree.

Secondly, the Christian Year needs to be re-established more thoroughly in our midst. The jettisoning of this, along with many other pious and seemly usages, on the part of the Puritans is now seen to have been too drastic, and many Congregationalists would admit that history has justified many of the arguments of Hooker in the Ecclesiastical Polity on such matters. The Puritans, in their spiritual strength, may not have needed the Christian Year in order to help them keep the proportion of faith but they should have avoided the typical error of over-zealous reformers and recognized that their children, who lack their zeal, might be grateful for its help. History has dealt very ironically with their refusal to see this, in that their children have re-introduced the Christian Year into their churches in such a way as to shock them far more than the Prayer Book would have done. For in many Congregational churches, as in many other churches, the re-introduction of the Christian Year has meant the observance of Christmas and Easter, but not that of Advent or Lent, of Pentecost but not of Ascensiontide and certainly not of that characteristically Reformed festival, Trinity Sunday. Those who wish to re-introduce a properly balanced Christian Year would be the first to insist that it be reformed and Biblical in character and free from liturgical preciosity. But they are surely equally right in protesting that to observe only those festivals which are popular holidays is to convict ourselves before the rest of the Church of spiritual triviality.

Finally, Congregationalists can learn from other churches about manners in church. Here again, the reaction against over-elaborate Popish ritual and undue attention to outward forms has led to the lack of ordered and seemly conventions of behaviour in church. This is accentuated in those churches, not perhaps so typical of Congregationalism as of some other bodies, whose origins were among simple people. Here the situation is one of confusion with the convention, in so far as it exists, in favour of the untidy and the casual. Thus, there is no doctrinal objection in Congregationalism to the practice of kneeling in prayer, as is indicated by the fact that it is customary, especially in the most old-fashioned churches, to kneel at a prayer-meeting in the vestry. Yet, the custom in church is, except in a growing minority of churches, against kneeling and people prefer the ungainly 'nonconformist crouch' even to the sober and primitive custom of standing for prayer. Likewise, manners at the Lord's Table frequently do not reach the level of refinement customarily to be found in private homes. Lady deacons, for example, are frequently not served first at the Lord's Table and the unsatisfactory, if theologically unobjectionable, practice of using individual communion cups often disturbs the service with clatter and raises embarrassing problems over their appropriate collection, while the design and workmanship of the vessels themselves are often unworthy of their solemn function. In all these matters, once more, the particularly seemly customs of the Church of England are ready to hand to guide us.

It will be clear that these points are not made as part of a self-conscious attempt to make Congregationalism more Anglican or more 'Catholic' in any denominational sense. It is true that the adoption of some of the suggestions of this chapter will bring us nearer to other churches but that, in itself, is a good thing and we all freely allow for the possibility that on some matters other churches may be right and we wrong. We have indeed a great deal to learn from other churches, and we can do so in a way which is faithful to that which is best in our own distinctive witness, if we understand our own position sufficiently well to see where what other churches have to teach best fits in. It is this which many Congregationalists today are trying to achieve, in churches which are unambiguously Congregationalist and try to emphasize the best of their own heritage but which are open to receive the best that others have to give and eager to emphasize their solidarity with all who bear the name of Christ. The ecumenical movement exists to help us become such churches and it is only as we move in this direction that we shall succeed in being faithful to Christ's purpose for His great Church in our own particular place.

VII

Manners and Morals

The question of the cultural impact made by churches upon their own members and upon society around them has received curiously little direct discussion. It is curious because it is obviously a matter of great importance and probably makes as much difference to the attractive or repulsive power of a particular church as anything it says in its overt teaching. As we partly indicated in the first chapter, the word 'culture' is used here in the sense with which Mr. T. S. Eliot has familiarized us in his *Notes towards the Definition of Culture*, to cover the total impression given by the manner of life of a group of people. In regard to churches, it covers not only their theology and devotion but also their style of architecture and interior decoration, their music and hymnology, their social life and economic organization and their distinctive habits of speech and dress.

Of course, all these attract a great deal of attention on semi-frivolous levels and there are many amateur students of denominational idiosyncrasies. Mr. John Betjeman has been heard to make the claim that he is able to tell the denomination of any particular chapel from a glance at its architecture and there are some who assert that they can immediately say which denomination a radio preacher comes from by listening to the tone of his voice. It has long been widely believed that the depth of a clergyman's collar in the Church of England provides a reliable guide to the height of his churchmanship, with the rule unexpectedly operating, 'The narrower the collar, the higher the churchmanship'. A few specialists have been able to pursue collar research further and to point out the partiality of British Fundamentalists for stiff white collars, of the more liberal Baptist ministers for semi-stiff white collars and of the older type of Congregationalist minister who reads idealist philosophy, quotes Browning and still supports the Liberal party, for wing-collars. And, of course, the mysterious provenance of clerical names has often fascinated observers, as is indicated by a famous discussion of the prevalence of triple-named ministers in churches on Manhattan Island in the *New Yorker* magazine some years ago, and by the delight with which the discovery of yet another Methodist Norman or Leslie or Anglo-Catholic Eric is greeted in some quarters. But all this lore exists chiefly on the level of common-room gossip. Few attempts have been made to relate it to wider questions of theology and morals.

When Congregationalism is looked at from this point of view, the first thing which becomes clear is that, both in England and America, it appears to lack a well-defined cultural attitude which marks it off sharply from other churches and from the rest of middle-class Anglo-Saxon society. In these days, it will require very great perception to discover without being told that a person one happens to meet in the ordinary way of business or social life is a Congregationalist. He might equally well be one type of Anglican or a Presbyterian, or, for that matter, any normal citizen of his own society. Congregationalism no longer possesses a distinctive and easily recognizable style.

To say this is not to imply that it is necessarily to be deplored. The word 'Nonconformist' conjures up, in the English mind in particular, an image which is far from being entirely pleasant. It suggests a combination of Dickens' Mr. Stiggins, an old-fashioned, unctuous grocer, and a worthy but dim female Sunday School teacher who serves behind the counter in the local Wool Shop. That image has always owed more to the snobbery and malice of the Anglican privileged classes of the nineteenth century, on whose heels the Nonconformists were pressing hard, than to close observation of reality. It was on a level of perversity comparable to that of Mr. Chesterton's poem on 'The Grocer and the Innkeeper' which proved only that Mr. Chesterton was not in the habit of doing the family shopping. Yet, of course, as with most caricatures, there was some element of truth in this picture and it is a matter of thankfulness that many of the factors which helped to give it what measure of plausibility it possessed have now been largely removed.

For one thing, the average level of education in Congregational churches is very much higher than it was a couple of generations ago. It is true that, as the knowledgeable Denis Brogan has observed, you will find very few Congregationalists or other Nonconformists who have been to Eton, but you will find an astonishingly large number who, by now, have been to universities of one kind or another, as the number of graduates who are now secretaries of Congregational churches prove.[1] In so far as the typical Congregationalist of the nineteenth century was a tradesman, and as we have seen that would be more likely to be the case in a small town than in a large city, he was a good tradesman, which meant that he prospered and gave his children a good education and probably turned them into professional men. Although a large proportion of the vast number of people to whom this

[1] Students of British social history will also be interested to know that at least three churches in the 1953 *Congregational Year Book* have colonels as their secretaries. The Secretary of a British Congregational church is an unpaid senior member of the diaconate, the equivalent of a Presbyterian session clerk. In America, the Church Secretary is frequently a salaried stenographer, and the member of the diaconate who performs functions similar to the British Church Secretary is normally called the Clerk.

has happened have been lost to Congregationalism in the process, especially if they went to Anglican public schools, a substantial number of them have obviously remained. The result has been that although, with a changing social structure, Congregationalism no longer possesses a group of outstanding laymen of great wealth and influence, the average level of education and general culture of congregations has risen, and with its rise a good deal of old-fashioned Nonconformist stuffiness and provincialism has disappeared, although it lingers still in some corners. And while many of the virtues of the older Congregationalist piety have vanished, some of its vices have vanished also. The preaching and public prayer in a modern Congregational church may often be regrettably tame and indeterminate but it will rarely be self-righteous and unctuous. Pompous oratory is in decline in our midst and the Nonconformist conscience is more frequently exercised in self-examination than in the dramatic denunciation of public sins of which no Nonconformist could conceivably be guilty.

There is no need for undue regret, therefore, at the passing of the old-fashioned Nonconformist style. The question remains, however, whether modern Congregationalism has anything in any way distinctive to put in its place. This question becomes the more disturbing when modern Congregationalism is compared, not with nineteenth-century Nonconformity, but with seventeenth-century Puritanism. For classical Puritanism undoubtedly had style. In architecture, dress, preaching, and psalmody it might be a severely plain style but in theology, philosophy, and poetry it most emphatically was not, although it contrived to remain culturally consistent throughout. Seventeenth-century Puritanism was, in many ways, as far removed from the popular Nonconformity of the nineteenth century as was Caroline Anglicanism from the Anglicanism of J. B. Dykes and fashionable Matins. In this respect, as in so many others, modern Congregationalism is far from being worthy of the best in its Puritan heritage. For the most part, it is barely distinguishable from any other respectable modern Protestant church which avoids undue eccentricities of taste or opinion. The opinions of most Congregational church members on matters of art, morals, or politics are not likely to be significantly different from those of most other fairly responsible and educated members of society. Anyone who is boldly original in these matters is as likely to find himself thrust to the margin of church life as he would be if he showed any startling originality in doctrine or devotional practice. Mr. Ivor Brown, in his *Winter in London*, described the character of Westcliff-on-Sea, near Southend, a typical seaside suburb of London, as being strictly Home Service, with rare excursions into the Light Programme and even rarer into the Third. That would stand for Congregationalism also, which, significantly has one of its most vigorously flourishing churches at Westcliff-on-Sea.

Now the Home Service has many virtues and so has middlebrow Congregationalism, virtues which, as we have seen, may easily be overlooked by self-centred highbrows looking for a church which will provide a suitable background to their own carefully contrived personalities. This is particularly true on the moral side, where Congregationalism's achievements are much more considerable than on the artistic. The specific guidance given by Congregational churches to their members on moral issues is frequently exiguous. Their embarrassment in dealing with questions of law and the difficulties they experience in laying down regulations which will be readily accepted by all churches prevent their giving to their members the clear guidance in regard to many matters of sex, business conduct and political and ecclesiastical duty which some other churches, notably of the Catholic type, are able to give. In many ways this works to their detriment yet it has not prevented them from fostering among their members a diffused ethical seriousness which often leads them to do justly and love mercy and walk humbly with their God in ways which put some churches of more scrupulous conscience to shame.

The ordinary Protestant churches have come in for a great deal of criticism in recent years, both from Catholics and secularists, on moral grounds. Catholics, with their genius for trying to have it both ways, have tended to criticize them for two contradictory reasons. They have accused Protestants of laxity in Christian discipline, reflected in carelessness over conditions of membership and lack of moral rigour in personal life, especially in connection with birth control and divorce, and of general assimilation to the spirit of the world. At the same time, they have accused Protestants of legalism, of exaggerated anxiety over the drinking and gambling habits of the populace, of a timid and censorious attitude towards the dance and the theatre, of tithing the mint and anise of personal and social behaviour while they neglect the weightier matters of the law. There is some justice in the former charge. What justice there is in the latter charge specifically in relation to Congregationalism will be considered later in this chapter. What is manifestly unjust is the failure which lies behind these criticisms to recognize the extent to which the world has been drawing and almost living upon the moral capital of popular Protestantism in the last couple of generations. For it is those countries dominated by popular Protestantism and that Anglicanism which is in so many ways related to it which have been the stoutest champions of human freedom and the most fruitful sources of works of compassion and of healing in the troubled days through which we have lived since the beginning of the first World War. Without seeking to disparage the noble and disinterested work of many Roman Catholic missions, where, except in Britain, America and a few similar Protestant countries, do you have an immediate and overwhelming popular response of help to those overtaken by calamity? The British and American public may often be defective in imagination and may occasionally fall into cruelty and injustice through short-sightedness or carelessness but they are not notably deficient in compassion. And, if it be granted that the commercial civilization of the Anglo-American world has many defects, in what countries of the world do the poorer workers enjoy a higher standard of living and where are standards of integrity and good workmanship higher? It would be absurd to claim that this is all due to the work of the Protestant Free Churches and it is obviously invidious to make comparisons of this kind between one country and another, but so much is made of these charges against Protestantism by Catholic apologists that it is sometimes necessary to call attention to the other side of the story. For example, Catholicism has often been presented as the bulwark of Christendom against Communism in the modern world, without any recognition of the fact that it is those countries which have Free Church Protestant majorities which present the strongest resistance to Communism because they have sufficient social health to prevent its taking serious hold. The influence of the Free Churches in producing this state of affairs is greater than might appear because they have encouraged their members to work through the ordinary agencies of secular society rather than through organizations bearing an ecclesiastical label.

Further, in a world of gigantic standing armies and concentration camps, of mutual exploitation by political groups and commercial enterprises, and of the feverish and restless pursuit of selfish pleasure by rootless and irresponsible masses, it may be possible to evaluate more justly than has been the case in the past, the magnitude of the moral achievement represented by the Free Churches of the Congregational type. Those voluntary societies of men and women united for no other purpose than the glory of God and their mutual benefit and the service of their neighbours, make no demand, whether financial or otherwise, upon the communities which they serve and seek only opportunities to help. To their own children, hankering after livelier and more diversified experiences than they can usually provide, they may sometimes seem dull and flat. It is true that the complacency which affects all successful organizations has gravely weakened them. But when their children rightly complain about their defects, they do well not to forget that to those who come into them from a harsh and alien world, as refugees from corrupt and tyrannous régimes, they seem almost like heaven itself, so full are they of the gentle and the kind and the good.

Even if all this is allowed, however, account must still be given of the alleged bourgeois mediocrity of so much of the life and witness of Congregational churches and the timid and repressive attitude towards such matters as drink, gambling, and sex with which Nonconformity is so notoriously associated. Much misunderstanding and even more prejudice becloud the popular vision over these matters and they are worth dwelling upon for a short time. First, in regard to sex, Congregationalism, although the same may not be true of some of the more conservative Protestant bodies, is now almost entirely free of the gloomy puritanical repressiveness of legend. It is far less puritanical than the Roman Catholic Church in this respect and indeed it exposes itself to the criticism that in some ways, in its distrust of celibacy, for example, it is not rigorous enough. As we have already seen, one of its greatest achievements has been in the encouragement of healthy and happy family life, although it has not escaped the dangers of a certain complacent domesticity in consequence. Congregationalists are apt to be much more legalistic in outlook over drink than over sexual matters, although this is by no means universally true, and, in these days, even more so over gambling than over drink, but there is very little fanaticism about them and the time-honoured suspicions of the theatre and the dance have long since disappeared. The amount of support that the Lord's Day Observance Society in England receives from Congregational sources is probably smaller than that which it receives from the Church of England.

The truth is that over many of these matters attitudes are conditioned as much by social as by theological factors. Continental Protestantism, which, on the whole, holds a theological position very similar to the Anglo-Saxon Free Churches, rarely sees any moral issue involved in taking alcoholic drink, except, of course, where it is taken to excess, and observes the 'Continental Sunday' as cheerfully as does Rome. On the other hand, Irish Roman Catholicism which is relatively complaisant over drinking and apparently enthusiastic over gambling maintains a strict protective legalism over sexual matters which makes the Scottish Wee Frees seem almost licentious. The reasons for these differences are various and may be partly fortuitous but they are clearly not all theological. As a rough generalization, it may be said that a church is likely to be the more puritanical the closer it is to the great, uneducated masses of the population because the need to give some order and discipline to lives which are not otherwise organized by social convention is so great. No one who has studied the effect of hard drinking on the industrial population of Victorian England or, for that matter, of gambling on the industrial population of modern England or the findings of the Kinsey Report, in so far as they can be relied upon when they are presented by researchers of such monolithic naïvety, on the sexual habits of the less educated section of the American public, will be readily disposed to deny that such rigorism is not sometimes necessary.

This is a point which needs to be borne in mind by those

Christians who find it easy to make fun of those who are earnestly scrupulous in relation to these matters. If a church does not need to show much strictness over questions like drink and the conventions governing relations between the sexes, it may be largely due to the fact that its influence is restricted to the sphere of those who may be assumed to have civilized habits in these respects and its members should understand the difficulties facing churches which might be very differently placed. At the same time, in situations where these difficulties are not serious, a rigorist attitude quickly becomes censorious and self-righteous and exposes itself to deserved ridicule. This is notoriously true in the case of aggressive teetotalism.

Conditions vary from one part of the world to another, but Congregational churches can claim to possess a fairly balanced attitude in respect of matters like this. Where they may be more defective is in their inability to bring a discriminating Christian judgment to bear on conventions of behaviour in a society which is becoming increasingly wealthy and 'cultured' in the narrow sense. Too many wealthy Congregationalists do not know what to do with themselves and either ape the manners and customs of sophisticated worldlings or else maintain an uninspired and unadventurous *petit bourgeois* simplicity which does little to enrich and enliven the common life or to set social standards. This problem is peculiarly acute in America, where Congregational churches can do far more than they are accustomed to do to set standards of social life which are free from snobbery, extravagance and ostentation but which yet represent a rich sense of the splendour, dignity, and beauty of human life.

An examination of the relation between Congregationalism and the arts provides a very good illustration of its strength and weakness in this realm. It has to be acknowledged that the contribution of Congregationalism to major artistic achievement has been very slight, except for poetry and hymnology. Its record in the visual arts is particularly poor. A few simple and pleasant seventeenth-century and Georgian churches and some fairly impressive Corinthian and Victorian Gothic façades, which are not to everyone's taste, in the nineteenth century in England, and a large crop of seemly and graceful Colonial churches in New England, practically sum up our architectural heritage. A few of the great English painters and musicians may have had Congregational connections but none of them have contributed anything distinctive to church life. In letters the record is much better. Leaving theology and preaching aside, Milton, Watts, and Browning stand out as our leading poets in England, and Defoe as a prose-writer. In New England, it may not be inappropriate, since the appearance of Perry Miller's biography,[1] to include Jonathan Edwards among the artists, and the 'flowering of New England' culture of the nineteenth century was the product of a Congregational milieu, even though much of it was not directly ecclesiastical in inspiration and it is debatable how much of it was Christian in character.

The reasons for this relative indifference to all the arts except literature may again be as much sociological as theological. Of course, theological factors are involved. The fact that theology encouraged plainness and simplicity in church design and ornament and disapproved of visual representation of the Deity gave little stimulus to the development of the visual arts, and the emphasis on preaching and theology and hymn-singing stimulated poetry and letters. But the lack of any noticeable interest in the visual arts among Congregationalists, as among other Free Churchmen, owed as much to the circumstances in which they were placed as to any theological views they held. Certainly it cannot be due solely

[1] *Jonathan Edwards* (Norton, 1952, the American Men of Letters Series).

to the alleged lack of an 'incarnational theology' on their part, as Catholic writers are disposed to claim in these days. The Dutch Reformed churches of the seventeenth century had a substantially similar theology to the English Congregationalists but that did not prevent the immense achievements of Dutch painting and the building up of the greatest artistic treasury since the Italian Renaissance.

The probability is that the lack of considerable artistic achievements among Congregationalists in England owes a great deal to the fact that for long generations they were a persecuted minority who were resolutely shut out from the national life. This did not prevent them from maintaining a strong educational influence through their academies, but it gave them few outlets for artistic interest, especially in relation to the visual arts, and when they were able to move out into the wider national life, their chief strength came to lie in the new industrial and commercial classes, who were not naturally disposed to artistic activity by their interests or their environment. It is, however, greatly to be regretted that there was such a weak tradition in the visual arts in Nonconformity in the nineteenth century because it was in that period that most of the large industrial and commercial cities and towns of England were built, with results which depress us to this day.

At the same time, this only too obvious fact should not conceal from us the other fact that, on many other levels, the cultural influence of nineteenth-century Congregational churches on the ordinary life of England was singularly beneficent and widespread. Once again, the familiar rule holds that in metropolitan circles the cultural influence of Congregationalism was negligible, but in the middle-class London suburb, or in the Midland or Northern industrial city or, above all, in the mining valley of Wales, the Congregational church was frequently by far the most important centre of literary and intellectual activity in the whole community. The pulpit appealed to the head as well as to the heart. It encouraged those in the pews to read and trained them in looking responsibly at public issues. The literary and debating societies which clustered busily around Congregational churches and met in their capacious halls gave their first taste of the literary and philosophical life to keen young people who were denied entry to the great public schools and universities. There are many people alive today who are proud to describe the Congregational church of their boyhood as 'their university'. The section on the churches in Booth's *Life and Labour of the People in London* at the turn of the century indicates how much solid substance there was in the claim. Even today, in this age of broadcasting and subsidized art clubs and evening classes on every conceivable subject, it is remarkable how much of the cultural activity of an ordinary English neighbourhood still flows through the organizations connected with the Congregational church, as is indicated by the list of voluntary clubs and organizations in High Wycombe prepared by Rowntree and Lavers in their *English Life and Leisure*.

When a Congregationalist moves out of the circle of local cultural life, Congregationalism quickly ceases to be of much help to him, and he moves either into Anglicanism or Romanism or into indifference or hostility to the churches. Whether any church could have kept in touch with D. H. Lawrence is doubtful but it is clear that his Congregationalism ceased to have any significant influence upon him as soon as he left Nottinghamshire. The positive effect of First Congregational Church, Oak Park, Illinois, upon Ernest Hemingway appears to have been even more vestigial. Even Robert Browning is not quite the exception in this respect that he might otherwise appear to be. Browning was a Camberwell Dissenter in the life of whose family the local Congregational church played a very important part. His wife was also a Congregationalist and both remained loyal to the church of their origins throughout their lives. Browning also received an unusually large amount of admiration and appreciation in Congregational circles. Yet he appears to have had few friends of his own persuasion who could give him the intellectual and spiritual companionship which might have fertilized his poetry, and it is significant that, like many American men of letters of similar background, he found it desirable to spend so much time abroad, in the midst of a culture startlingly unlike his own. The fact that Browning is the nearest approach to a successful and representative man of letters that British Congregationalism possesses is an indication of the problems confronting the serious artist in a Congregationalist setting.

What has been true of England has been even more strikingly true of America, where the opportunities of cultural leadership for Congregationalism have been so much greater. Congregationalism may claim to have taken the lead in laying the foundation of the educational structure of the country, and the emphasis on education which spread from New England out through the Middle West has undoubtedly been one of the main sources of modern America's strength. Many of the artistic and intellectual leaders of America right down to our own day have received their initial cultural impulse through Congregational churches and through colleges of Congregational foundation. Many of the colleges, in particular, retain a position of cultural leadership. The Congregational influence in them is, however, by now frequently so diffused as to be almost undetectable. Even as far back as the second half of the nineteenth century, Congregationalism was showing little ability to give much prophetic guidance to the cultivated minds of New England, and it is significant that where the artistic and intellectual leaders of America have not been heretics or unbelievers they have found more inspiration in Episcopalian or Roman Catholic circles than in Congregational. Its failure to speak a distinctive word on the cultural problems of the modern world has meant that Congregationalism has lost many of its own best children.

How is the situation to be improved? This is a question which is exercising the minds of an increasing number of Congregationalists today. It is clear that a deliberate attempt to encourage the cultivation of the arts in Congregationalism as it is at present will do little good and might do much harm. We have already had examples of experiments in religious drama and pageantry and essays in architecture and ritual which, with a few exceptions, do little more than reflect the lack of vitality of our tradition in these matters. The new interest in the study and painting of chapels which exists in fashionable artistic circles today is on a different level but it also carries its own dangers. Messrs. Betjeman and Piper, who have taken a lead in expressing such an interest, are sympathetic and perceptive Christians, but others who lack their background may be encouraged by their example to start a cult of chapels and chapel culture as something 'quaint' and 'amusing'. Congregationalism will make no progress in the arts until it ceases to be either.

A true revival of the arts in Congregationalism can only come as the fruit of a religious and theological revival, which carries with it a new conviction of the wonder and majesty of God and of the world which He addresses and renews in Christ. The relation between great art and great religion and theology is not immediate or simple but in the long run it is decisive. In the present cultural situation of Congregationalism it is likely to be much more direct than it frequently is. Theological revivals do not necessarily produce great art and, even when they do, it generally takes at least a generation for the new outlook to express itself in artistic terms, but, where favourable social and educational conditions exist as well, they are likely to do so. To say that the conditions exist for a great artistic revival in modern Congregationalism would be to go absurdly beyond the evidence, especially in regard to the visual arts. But it is not too much to say that the revival of Protestant theology, in which our churches have fully shared, combined with the rising standard of general education among their members and the interchange of experience among churches in the ecumenical movement, helps to produce a situation where, for once in our history, it is not fantastic to envisage the possibility of such conditions emerging.

VIII

Congregationalism and Secular Society

The subject of the relation between Congregationalism and secular society has received very little systematic discussion. This is true even of the situation in England and it is even more true of the larger and more complex American situation. Its discussion in this chapter will, therefore, have to be occupied chiefly with England and we can do no more than hope that it will stimulate someone to work along similar lines in relation to America.

The story of Congregationalism's relation to secular society follows very closely that which we have seen to hold for many other spheres of its life. In particular localities its influence has frequently been powerful and effective. In national and international life its influence has been inconspicuous and occasional. The reasons for this are to be found in the nature of Congregational church organization but, in England at least, they have been accentuated by the peculiar circumstances of our history.

After the collapse of their dream of a 'godly commonwealth' in England and the Restoration of 1660, most Congregationalists, along with other Dissenters, were forced into social obscurity where they did not actually 'go underground'. Yet, despite all the restrictions on their activities, which were only partly removed by the Revolution of 1688 and whose re-imposition was averted only by the death of

Queen Anne, it was not long before they began to play an influential part in the affairs of the cities and towns of England. Already in the eighteenth century, the dissenting merchants were becoming mayors and lord mayors and, as Bernard Manning has shown,[1] those of London in particular were beginning to show exceptional political skill in looking after the well-being of Dissenters in society. It was not until the nineteenth century, however, that their influence frequently became dominant. Dissenters were the moving spirits in the foundation of the fortunes of many of the industrial cities of England, with Congregationalists prominent among them, and they naturally moved into positions of civic leadership. This was most obvious in the Midlands and the North but it was also more true than is often realized in East Anglia and in those market towns of the South and West which experienced a measure of industrial development in the nineteenth century. Further, although it is widely assumed that the connection between Congregationalism and local government which was built up in this way has largely been broken, this is by no means entirely true. There are Congregational churches in the provincial towns of England which continue to be known as the churches of the mayors and it still sometimes happens that the Lord Mayor of London is a Congregationalist. The connection is certainly not as emphatic or as self-conscious as it was but it remains clearly visible.

These Congregationalist mayors were, for the most part, manufacturers or prominent tradesmen. As tradesmen they would be more likely to be drapers than the grocers of popular legend and, in course of time and as their towns expanded, they frequently blossomed out as owners of the chief local department store. It would be an interesting piece of minor research to discover how many Congregationalist deacons of the last fifty or sixty years were the founders of department

[1] In *The Protestant Dissenting Deputies* (Cambridge, 1952).

stores and how many of them became mayors or aldermen. A fair sprinkling of these Congregationalist mayors were, however, professional men, chiefly solicitors, and increasingly included many representatives of the new professional groups such as accountants and estate agents. Standing behind them and influencing their opinions on political matters almost as much as their ministers, and sometimes a good deal more, was the editor of the local Liberal paper. He is a person, very frequently both a Congregationalist and a man of considerable culture, whose social and political importance has never received the attention it deserved, very curiously in such an articulate profession. The importance of similar people in America, also frequently Congregationalists, has been more widely recognized. The ranks of such men are sadly diminished in these days of a centralized and sensationalist press, but there are still some to be found, especially in the North of England, who vigorously maintain a brave tradition and, while the *Manchester Guardian* flourishes, they will feel that their cause is not entirely lost.

As the nineteenth century went on into the twentieth, it became increasingly clear that this group was in a position to be a major force in national politics. They were the natural leaders of the most progressive sections of the community in the industrial towns and cities of Britain and it was in these towns and cities that the nation was expanding most rapidly. The number of Nonconformists in Parliament steadily grew and, as their numbers and power developed, they found the burdens imposed upon them by the privileged position of the Established Church increasingly intolerable. The time came when they found themselves strong enough to fight to cast off these burdens and this they did with considerable success. Most religious tests were removed, the Church in Ireland was disestablished, to be followed by the disestablishment of the Church in Wales, and there was serious talk of rude hands being laid upon the Church of England itself. Meanwhile, determined efforts were made to shake the Anglican hold on the schools and there were lively fights over the Education Acts of 1904. When the Liberals enjoyed their great triumph in 1906, it was widely acknowledged that the shock troops of victory were the Nonconformists, and among the politically-minded Nonconformists the Congregationalists were outstanding. The record of that government was in many respects notable and it holds the distinction of having laid the foundation for many of the social services we enjoy today. What the shape of modern England would have become if it had been allowed to develop according to the logic of the pre-1914 situation is an interesting but vain speculation. Certainly, there were many social forces operative in it which were very different from those normally thought of when the memory of Edwardian days is evoked. But 1914 came and the war threw the elements of the British situation into confusion and brought entirely new forces into operation. The results were grave enough for Congregational churches, but for the Liberal party through which they found their chief political expression they appear to have been disastrous.

The political history of the last fifty years in relation to the churches has yet to be adequately studied. It will present a fruitful field to the discriminating student. Until such students appear, any generalizations which can be made about it must be very tentative and vague. Yet generalizations must be made, for without them it is impossible to obtain much light on the extremely difficult, complicated, and neglected question of the duty of Congregationalism in its distinctiveness in present-day politics.

A reaction has recently set in among Congregationalists against the veneration in which their political activities up to 1914 used to be held. This reaction has found its chief expression in Dr. H. F. Lovell Cocks' scintillating little book, *The*

Nonconformist Conscience,[1] in which he exposes the mock heroics of a good deal of Nonconformist political campaigning in the years before 1906, the short-sightedness of their educational policy and their fatal tendency to over-simplify issues by the use of pompous slogans such as, 'What is morally wrong can never be politically right' and applying them inappropriately to such matters as the Parnell case. The reaction is necessary and salutary, if only because it reveals some of the causes of our present political decline. Yet it should not hide from us the magnitude of the political achievement of our fathers or the extent to which we are in poorer case than they.

First, whatever else might be said about them, they did have a real effect upon politics. The churches today are much more vocal and in some ways much better informed on political matters than they used to be, but it is all chiefly on the level of principle. Their political action is more often a matter of what the bishops say than of what Christians in politics actually do. There was a time, and it was not so long ago, when Congregationalist church deacons and members, and sometimes ministers as well, could make up their minds on an issue and know where to go to ensure that their minds could be expressed with the greatest possible cogency and effectiveness. They often made up their minds in a way which may fill us today with misgivings, but any criticism we make of them must be tempered by the recognition that we have bought our more detached and balanced outlook at the price of political ineffectiveness.

Secondly, not all their actions were misconceived. It is sometimes implied today by Catholic apologists who are sharply critical of the movement of modern society that the Industrial Revolution was the product of Nonconformists or at least Puritans and that its evils reflect their mentality.

[1] Independent Press, London, 1944.

Certainly, they played a very great part in its development and must bear their share of the blame for its evils. But any criticism of them must be tempered by the recognition that they were also among its earliest, sternest, and most effective critics and that, long before Catholic converts living in Ditchling and Chipping Campden awoke to the evils of industrialism, Congregationalist manufacturers, editors, and ministers, living in Birmingham, St. Helens, and Batley were at work striving to civilize and humanize the Industrial Revolution. Everyone except a Labour candidate at an election knows that the foundations of modern welfare legislation were laid in the nineteenth and early twentieth centuries. The part played by Nonconformists, among whom Congregationalists as well as Quakers were prominent, in promoting the voluntary activity on which such legislation was based is not so well known. Their knowledge of industrial society and their comparative freedom from class-consciousness as well as their reformist zeal have been among the chief sources of the most solid and useful forms of social service in modern England.

Thirdly, political Nonconformity can make out a case for itself even over those matters where it is now most widely criticized, its attitude to the relation between church and state and education. We can now see that, in their agitation for disestablishment and in their truculent insistence on the 'secularization' of public education, Nonconformists were taking it for granted that the substructure of the life of the community would remain consciously Christian and that the activities of the state could continue to be severely restricted, and we can also see that such assumptions revealed a serious failure in prophetic understanding. Nevertheless, as Dr. A. R. Vidler has recognized in his study of W. E. Gladstone in *The Orb and the Cross*, such notions must have presented themselves with a very considerable degree of plausibility in the years from 1870 to 1914. The demons we have known had not then been unleashed over our world and men secure in their conviction of their ability to sustain their own churches in responsible freedom could concentrate their attention on the manifest injustices of the church establishments in Ireland and Wales and on the highly unsatisfactory nature of the establishment in England. And while their notion, which is still widely maintained in America, that it is possible to have a comprehensive education which is religiously neutral was dangerously naïve and did a great deal of damage to the educational structure of our country which is only now in slow process of repair, they can claim, at least, that the relaxation of clerical control over schools was necessary and has been most beneficial to the whole status and sense of vocation of the teaching profession. Besides, none of the churches, either alone or together, could have undertaken or even directed the vast programme of school building and expansion which was necessary if the rapidly increasing population of Britain was to be educated. It is, admittedly, a disconcerting fact that until the advent of the Agreed Syllabus, few constructive suggestions were made by Nonconformists about how schools might remain Christian while being freed from clerical control, but perhaps events have broadly justified their contention that schools do not necessarily become less Christian in tone and teaching when they are released from direct ecclesiastical influence.

Another point in the favour of the political activities of Congregationalism before 1914 is that it frequently had a more creative attitude towards the rise of the Labour movement than it is commonly supposed to have had today. It is true that in many neighbourhoods the old jibe that Congregational churches were committee rooms for the Liberal party had a good deal of justification, but this was by no means universally so. If it was Methodism which was the great force behind Trade-Unionism in the North-east, the Congregational churches provided a fair amount of its leadership in many of the smaller industrial towns of the Midlands and South Wales, and the connection is still discernible. Also, although it might often happen that the local 'Socialist intellectual' school teacher in a particular place would be strenuously opposed to the church in all its forms, it might equally frequently be the case that he would be found as an active member and office-bearer in the Congregational church. It should also be remembered that, in those larger Congregational churches whose leaders might be solidly Liberal in politics, there would be a Brotherhood or a Debating Society or a Young Men's Class which provided a sphere of training and a reasonably sympathetic platform for many who became leaders of the Labour movement. It is not an accident that so many Congregational church members found it easy to shift their allegiance from the Liberal to the Labour party with the re-arrangements of party power after the two World Wars.

But, even though all this is freely acknowledged, there is no denying the fact that the catastrophic decline of Liberalism and of political Nonconformity has presented modern Congregationalism with problems concerning the fulfilment of its political responsibilities which are extremely hard to define, let alone to solve. For example, it is hard to see how Congregationalism can aspire again to speak with a distinctive and united voice on any long-term political issue. Churches may still unite to pass resolutions and influence opinion over very clear and strictly limited moral issues, but it is unlikely that the Dissenting Interest, with its own well-defined position on major matters of national policy of which all politicians have to take some cognizance, will ever again be a relatively permanent factor in British politics. The reasons for this are not due merely to the weakness of our churches or to the inadequacy of our political spokesmen. They are also due to radical changes in the relation of churches to each other and of all churches to society and to the new social and political alignments created by the rise of organized Labour. The Dissenting Interest is, in fact, no longer a coherent interest, in the political sense, and it is quite vain artificially to try to recreate it.

In itself, of course, this is by no means a bad thing. It means that Congregationalists should be able to achieve a more objective approach to social and political matters and speak as one group among the churches, enjoying the benefit of the experience and wisdom of other churches, which may serve to correct any distortion of vision of their own. Anyone who considers how often churches have failed to give prophetic leadership to the nation as a whole in the past because they have been suspicious of each other cannot but be thankful for the inter-denominational character of much of the guidance given to churches on social and political matters today. All the same, particular denominations still have their links and associations with particular policies, groups and parties, and they still have a measure of responsibility to the whole witness of the Church to ensure that they handle these in the most useful ways. It is at this point that it becomes peculiarly hard to see how Congregationalists should conduct themselves in the present situation.

First, a substantial number of Congregationalists remain in the Liberal party and have a historic responsibility to the concerns and organization of that party. Several of its leaders are active members of Congregational churches and are, presumably, in a good position to influence its policies. Whether their Congregationalism has been a partial source of weakness to them in encouraging a certain individualism without reference to harsh political realities which may have helped to make the debacle of the party so great in the last twenty-five years is an interesting speculation but one which it would be difficult to substantiate. What is much clearer is that the leaders of thought in Congregationalism have shown a curious indifference to the fate of the Liberal party, even though it has meant the virtual disfranchisement of many of their church members, and have made very little attempt to help it re-think its basis or regain political effectiveness. By now it may be too late to make such an attempt. That in itself is a matter of debate and the present writer is not competent to make a judgement upon it. But, whether it be done through a revival of the Liberal party or not, Congregational churches still have every reason to be concerned whether their people are making the kind of impact upon politics which adequately expresses that which is most distinctive in their own outlook.

For example, with the decline of the Liberal party a large number of Congregationalists have joined the Conservative party. No statistics are available on this point, of course, but there can be little doubt that the strength of the Conservative party in Congregationalism has greatly increased in recent years. In itself, this is natural and probably inevitable, and only the most passionate adherent of the rival parties would be disposed to regard it as a bad thing. By economic interest and social outlook, perfectly proper factors in determining political loyalties under a democratic party system, many Congregationalists now belong to the conservative section of society and it is only to be expected that they should join the Conservative party. Whether the way in which they have done so is a good thing, however, is much more doubtful. For when Congregationalists have become Conservatives they have done so uncritically, without raising the question of how their Conservatism should differ from that of others, who have reached their position by very different roads. Thus, understandably enough, few Congregationalists appear to have become Tories, High Church and strong supporters of the Landed Interest, but they have not made any attempt to re-define Conservatism in such a way as to include the witness of the modern representatives of classical Dissent and Liberalism, and they have certainly received no encouragement from their intellectual leaders to do so. For the most part they have, in a depressing way, contrived only to absorb the outlook of the ever-growing commercial and financial wing of the Conservative party, while losing something of the open-mindedness and sensitive social conscience which their fathers with similar interests possessed in the heyday of the Liberal party.

A very good illustration of the transformation which has overtaken many of the more prosperous families of Congregational origin is provided by the story of the Berry family of Merthyr Tydfil. It is, perhaps, not inappropriate to mention them by name because the two most prominent members of the family are devoted to the cause of publicity and to the influencing of opinion. It would be hard to find a more typical example of a Congregational family of a generation ago than this. The father of the famous trio of Berry brothers was a reasonably successful and highly respected business man in Merthyr Tydfil, a deacon of the English Congregational Church and in his time mayor of the town. As is often the way with such families, all three sons became extremely successful men of business. The two who need concern us here, William and Gomer, went into printing and the newspaper world, where they achieved very great fame and fortune as the press magnates, Lords Camrose and Kemsley. In the process, however, they shed all distinctive marks of their Congregationalism, at least as far as the policy of their newspapers was concerned, and contented themselves with being the spokesmen of modern big business Conservatism. Even when they took over a paper of Liberal tradition, the *Sunday Times*, they gradually transformed it into a paper of this type, so that the formerly Conservative *Observer*, partly perhaps through the influence of more faithful Nonconformists of the older generation like Isaac Foot and Tom Jones, took over the succession of nineteenth-century Liberalism. The chief property of the Kemsley empire, the *Daily Telegraph*, is a most efficiently run and readable paper, and it is sympathetic enough to churches in a general way. No one could describe it as being representative of either the good or the ill of the Congregationalist tradition. Yet it is probably the paper which is most widely read in those neighbourhoods where Congregational churches are strongest.

It has already been hinted that the relation between Congregationalism, despite its middle-class character, and the Labour party is stronger than it is commonly supposed to be. At least two Congregationalists were members of the Cabinet in the last Labour Government and there are many Congregationalist Labour Members of Parliament, one of them a well-known Welsh preacher. Yet here, again, there is little evidence of any attempt to work out a relation between Congregational teaching and Socialism. The editor of the *New Statesman*, the opinion-forming weekly journal of the Left, is Kingsley Martin, the son of a Congregational minister, but, although his writings occasionally reveal a curiously ambivalent attitude towards his Christian and Nonconformist background, he can hardly be considered as representative of any aspect of modern Congregationalist Socialism. The field is wide open today for a reinterpretation of the aims and ideals of British Socialism. Congregationalists might be considered to be among those who were well fitted to embark on such a reinterpretation, since there are many among them who are kindred spirits to leaders of the older generation of leaders of Socialist thought like Lindsay and Tawney, of whom it could be said that, although neither of them happened to be Congregationalists, both might easily have been. There is, however, very little sign at present of any great readiness to seize the opportunity.

Congregationalism has to confess, therefore, that it shares to the full the uncreative approach to modern British politics which is characteristic of most of the churches today, despite the fact that an unusually large number of convinced Christians are to be found in positions of political leadership. If it is no worse than other churches in this respect, it is not very obviously better, and it has peculiar problems to face arising out of the decline of the Liberal party. It has already been suggested that, in regard to most matters, Congregationalism's approach to politics is not likely to differ greatly henceforward from that of the other major churches. There are, however, a few directions in which it seems clear that it should be able to make a distinctive and positive contribution which might be of benefit to all churches and to secular society itself.

First, Congregationalists can at least ensure that that which has been their greatest contribution to social health in the past—their emphasis on the local community—is able to continue to be made in the future. Many things militate against the growth of strong local communities in these days, the rapidity and ease of modern transport, the mobility of industry, the concentration of life in great metropolitan centres. Yet it remains true that it is only in the situation where the human measure is observed and where the dignity and distinctiveness of human relations receive due attention that men can effectively learn the art of living together in society. All students of modern society see the need of this, but it will not be done if it is done only out of a sense that it is socially desirable. The movement of the times is against it. It will be done only if a renewed conviction of the grace and love of God prompts men to join themselves into church order with their neighbours. Congregationalists should understand this better than any other Christian group and see the vital social importance of building up local churches. Without them, the very living tissue of society itself is not healthily formed and the vast, shapeless conurbations of modern times present a terrifying spectacle of potential corruption. Indeed, as we all know, in many lands this corruption has become an accomplished fact. If Methodism saved England from political revolution at the time of the Industrial Revolution, the presence of vigorous churches of Congregationalist type in the residential and suburban areas of England and America may build up reservoirs of social health which will resist the diseases of Fascism and its allies, which breed rapidly in such areas in periods of radical social adjustment.

Secondly, Congregationalism will not be able to make much of a contribution along these lines even on the local level if it fails to reorganize itself more effectively to meet and overcome the problems with which the centralizing tendency of modern life confronts it. For, unless there is free circulation between the life of the locality and the larger society, the most intensive cultivation of the local situation is likely to breed only frustration. In the past, churches have given a great deal of guidance to secular society, often quite unconsciously, about how to solve some of its most intractable problems. It is widely recognized that one of the greatest problems of our day is that of 'democracy face to face with hugeness', of how to retain genuine personal responsibility and initiative in a society so large and complex that it is often almost impossible to define responsibility or express initiative. The churches can help up to a point by clarifying principles and giving good advice to the state and to the representatives of local government. But their most valuable help will be given if they can demonstrate that they have solved this problem in their own internal life. It has already been said that Congregational churches can hardly claim to have done so. Until they can do so, much of their witness on behalf of political as well as ecclesiastical freedom will inevitably sound as mere verbiage in the ears of their contemporaries.

Thirdly, in the modern world Congregationalists need to revise their ideas of the relation between church and state. Most people see that in a situation like the present, where the state is taking over the control and organization of more and more of life, it is increasingly impossible for the state and the churches to have a merely neutral attitude towards each other and resolve each to go its own way. Congregationalists, in common with many other Free Churchmen, now frequently acknowledge that in England simply to press for the disestablishment of the Church of England is an inadequate way of dealing with the problem. Free Churches themselves receive indirect forms of aid from the state. The state itself shows an obstinate tendency, for which there is a great deal of practical justification, to treat with all the churches, whether established or free, as a single group over many matters of mutual interest, of which the classic example is that of War Damage Compensation. And Free Churchmen wish to do nothing to weaken Christian influence in the councils of the nation, recognizing, as their fathers did not always succeed in doing, that the Christian foundation of our nation's life can no longer be taken for granted. Their objection to the unsatisfactory form of the present establishment in England is, therefore, tempered by their realization that a new relationship between all the main churches and the state will have to be worked out, in which the churches must strive to reach agreement among themselves in their dealings with the state.[1] This is a great step forward, but it still leaves unanswered the further question of how Christian people are to help the state, in democracies like Britain and America, to reach a Christian understanding of itself. Congregationalist thought has been singularly weak on this matter, partly because, as F. D. Maurice used to complain, it did not clearly express its belief

[1] See 'The Free Churches and the State', the Report of the Commission of the Free Church Federal Council, London, 1953.

in a spiritual constitution of the universe and, as P. T. Forsyth used to thunder, it had lost the note of public responsibility. Yet an answer to this question is more important than that of the general relation between the churches and the state because it directly affects the matter of the aims and context of education, which in these days has become a major concern of the state. Congregationalists both in the British Commonwealth and in the U.S.A. must strive, in concert with other churches, to answer this question if they are to speak a relevant word to secular society today.

American Congregationalism possesses an institution, the Council for Social Action, which has no equivalent in British Congregationalism, and which acts as an admirable instrument for educating members of Congregational churches in relation to their duty in society. This Council has its own staff and periodical, and produces guidance for the churches on many important issues which reaches a high level of competence. The Council has come in for some criticism, chiefly from laymen and ministers who do not share the views on political and economic matters frequently expressed in Council publications. Most of these criticisms have been shown to be unfounded. At the same time, American Congregationalism will have to ask itself whether it has paid enough attention to the kind of issues which have been discussed in this chapter in their British setting. In particular, it is strange that, in a country which leads the world in sociological study, so little thought has been given to the question of how Congregational churches themselves, given their distinctive history and composition, can best influence the social and political life of their communities. The field would seem to be wide open for realistic thought and experiment in this matter.

IX

Prospect for Congregationalism

'The Spirit bloweth where it listeth', and the fortunes of churches can take the most unexpected and unaccountable turns, but this does not mean that in assessing the future prospects of churches we are left simply with the alternatives of vigilant agnosticism or optimistically pious generalization. The rise of the ecumenical movement, with its habit of looking at churches in relation to each other and of seeking to discern the movement of God's Spirit in the world at large, does enable us to consider probabilities in this realm more realistically than ever before. Of course, nothing like scientific accuracy in forecasting is either desirable or possible here, and anything which is attempted must be qualified by the cheerful recognition that an entirely unforeseen factor may enter the situation and that God may lead us into the completely unknown. Yet there are two fairly clear guiding principles which make an assessment of probabilities in this realm a little more than a matter of mere guesswork.

The first of these is that the condition of any particular church or denomination depends on the condition of other churches, both for good and evil, to a far greater extent than is commonly realized. The second is that the prosperity or otherwise of churches is closely related to the general social context in which the churches exist. That sounds very obvious, but it has implications which are not always clearly brought out.

Churches depend upon each other in numerous ways and

some of them have not yet been adequately studied. Perhaps the chief which need concern us as we consider the prospects for Congregationalism is the way in which churches depend upon each other for their supplies of new members. The number of converts a church makes from among the unchurched multitudes varies greatly with the character of the particular church. Broadly speaking, it can be said that the majority of churches in English-speaking lands recruit most of their members either from the families of existing members or by transfer, whether through change of residence or change of conviction, from other churches. The minority of whom this is not true are usually churches of the simple and poor, who concentrate most of their energies upon evangelism. In the past, most of these churches were of the Methodist or Baptist type, to be followed, as these stabilized and institutionalized themselves, by the Salvation Army. Nowadays, observation seems to suggest—and in the absence of definite statistics no statement can be more precise than that—that most of such churches are Protestant sects of a very primitive type and comparatively recent origin, the Pentecostals, the Assemblies of God, the Nazarenes and so on. Other churches attract their converts from outside the Christian family in small numbers but these must attract the majority of their members from outside, if only because the more settled churches provide a most unfruitful field for their evangelism.

Not many of these little churches are able, however, to keep their new-found members in their fold for very long, unless they themselves undergo considerable change. When their converts do not slip back to where they came from, one of two things is likely to happen to them. Either the church itself develops in maturity and spiritual understanding and becomes a respectable and recognized member of the family of churches, as several of the smaller Baptist denominations have, or else those who were converted by the raw and narrow sect move on, as their experience develops, to another and more spacious part of the Church. This may sometimes happen within the life-span of a particular individual but it more frequently happens within the experience of his children. A man of little education who has led a dissolute or purposeless existence has been converted by a sect which has preached to him a crude but powerful Gospel of personal decision. As a result of his conversion, his life acquires discipline and gradually his home acquires a measure of dignity. He is able to give his child a better upbringing than he himself received. The child will go to a better school than his father did and perhaps to college. The child will have received a vivid religious impression from his upbringing which nothing will be able to efface, but developing experience will make him increasingly dissatisfied with the church life which provided it. If he does not react against it altogether, he will begin to look around for a church with a conception of the Gospel and of the Christian life which he now finds more acceptable and, as soon as he is free to do so, he moves over to such a church.

This is the most typical form of religious migration in the English-speaking countries and the chief way in which new Christian families are brought into circulation among the churches, but there are other kinds. The person brought up in a very liberal church reacts against what he conceives to be the indefiniteness on religious superficiality of his environment into fundamentalism or, more commonly, into a form of Catholicism. The person brought up in a pious household which has been deeply involved in the life of a particular church often seems to find it necessary to make his spiritual home in another communion, perhaps in order to convince himself that his soul is his own. As a very rough generalization, it might be said that churches in the liberal Protestant tradition like the Congregationalist and many of the Methodist and Presbyterian churches flourish at the expense of the new sects or the more conservative Evangelical bodies, and that the more liturgically developed and aristocratic churches, like Anglicanism and the metropolitan forms of Roman Catholicism, flourish at the expense of these same Liberal Protestant churches.

It is admitted that more research must be done upon these matters before anyone can confidently assert that they are as they have been described, but enough evidence is available to prompt the churches towards a new humility in their dealings with each other. In particular, since churches are peculiarly disposed to be snobbish and indifferent towards each other, the more polished and respectable churches should realize much more vividly than they do the extent to which they depend upon the cruder and more aggressive churches and should find a new interest in studying them sympathetically. The prosperity of a particular church is intimately bound up with the success or failure of another church which might feed it or draw people away from it, and a church's prospects cannot be adequately assessed except in the setting of the movement of church life as a whole.

This is more true of Congregationalism than of many other churches, for it both receives and passes on members in a fairly large way. Indeed, from this point of view it may claim to be much more of a bridge-church, if that is at all a desirable thing to be, than the Church of England. It receives a steady stream of adherents from the more primitive and the more conservative churches. This is especially true of the U.S.A. A substantial part of the membership of a fashionable Congregational church in the suburb of a mid-Western city is likely to be made up of people who were brought up either in a narrowly Evangelical church of the type which abounds in America or else in a strongly conservative or clericalist church, which might be Lutheran or Roman Catholic. These people are attracted to the Congregational church when they move to the suburb, both because it is one of the major centres of religious and social life in its community and because they find its atmosphere either more spacious or more free than that of the church which they have left. Whether this migration is desirable or not, the facts that the churches from which these people come remain numerous and populous and that the movement continues of people from the countryside and down-town areas of big cities where those churches are to be found to the suburbs and pleasant residential quarters, suggest that American Congregational churches which are located in these neighbourhoods will continue to enjoy great prosperity. In England this trend is nothing like so pronounced but it certainly exists. The comparative prosperity which Congregational churches enjoy in new suburbs and seaside resorts is not due only to the transfer of members from other Congregational churches but also to the influx of recruits from churches of the type we have described. It is reasonable to suppose that this process will continue, but the fact that England lacks the immense reservoir of popular Protestantism upon which America is able to draw suggests that, as far as this source of new life is concerned, American Congregationalism will go on expanding more rapidly than that of England for a long time to come.

Our second guiding principle was that the prosperity or otherwise of churches was closely related to their general social setting. Here it can be said that some aspects of the general movement of society in the English-speaking countries are likely to create more favourable conditions for the growth of Congregational churches than they have known in the past. It is frequently observed in these days, generally by people who have a sense of their own superiority to their fellows and who deplore the tendency, that we are all in process of becoming one great lower-middle-class. It would be foolish to pretend that this does not entail losses and that it provokes many new dangers, not least for Congregationalism itself, but it should also produce many large-scale benefits, whose character is as yet barely visible, particularly for churches like Congregationalism. This is especially true in England, although it also has application in many parts of the U.S.A. as well.

We have seen that very few of the so-called working-classes are to be found in the churches. There are many reasons for this but one of the chief is undoubtedly that they have lacked the social confidence which would enable them to participate readily in the life of institutions which make heavy demands on their knowledge and their sense of responsibility. Where conditions enable them to have this social confidence, as in the countryside and industrial valleys of Wales, they belong to the churches in large numbers. A much higher minimum income, greater security of employment, and wider educational opportunities are bound slowly to increase the social confidence of large numbers of people who, at present, do not have any strong sense of playing any significant part in the general life of society. Can it not be argued that this will make them a little more ready to contemplate joining churches? This is an unfashionable line of argument in some quarters but surely ordinary observation of the movement of society, quite apart from any political overtones it might have, seems to suggest that there is some substance in it, however much it may need to be hedged about with qualifications. If the churches, for good or ill, flourish best among the middle-classes, and if strenuous efforts are being made to provide the whole population with what used to be considered as middle-class standards of income, education, housing, and health service, it is not unreasonable to hope that the social conditions which promote the emergence of prosperous churches will become much more widespread, both in town and country.

These considerations should, at least, provide Congregational churches, along with others, with a new impulse towards trying to deal with one of their most intractable problems. All the familiar difficulties involved in appealing to simple people who are ruled by conventions which find little place for church-going remain and they are intensified by the prevailing mood of restlessness and superficiality, but the fact that social circumstances have changed to this extent in their favour is a challenge to Congregationalists to make new efforts, for example, to evangelize the young families of working-class background who are gathering in the new housing estates and who are likely, in many cases, to have a different outlook on life from their parents. In England at present, it is the Church of England which is in the best position to make the most of this opportunity because its organization permits it to have men available quickly to work in these areas. If it continues to work in the direction of building up parish meetings and encouraging lay initiative it may be adequate to the task but most of its leaders would cordially agree that because, on the whole, the Free Churches have a more effective tradition of work in working-class neighbourhoods, the work of the Church of England needs badly to be strengthened and supplemented by that of the Free Churches. The churches are, of course, fully alive to their responsibilities in this realm and their eagerness to work is limited only by the difficulty of obtaining buildings, leadership and resources with which to begin, but to realize the way in which social circumstances have begun to move in our favour may help to spur us to greater effort.

Congregational churches are alive to their responsibilities in this realm, both in England and America, even though they may have great difficulty in fulfilling them. It is doubtful, however, whether there is the same awareness of their responsibilities at the other end of the social and educational scales.

Yet Congregationalism loses, as it has over several generations, many of its most privileged and best educated children to other churches and is likely to continue doing so unless it makes new efforts to keep them. The extent of these losses is partly concealed by the natural and unobtrusive way in which they happen, so that we are half-consciously resigned to them and conclude that there is nothing that we can do about them. In the nineteenth century and up to 1914, many people left Congregationalism in England because their wealth or their education made them aspire to be accounted among the 'ruling classes' or the gentry and these were, almost to a man and a woman, Anglican. That attitude, and the situation which produces it, has not entirely disappeared and they are still found in surprising purity and strength in some of the quieter corners of so fanatically conservative a country as England but, for obvious reasons, it is in general nothing like so strong as it used to be. The losses of the sophisticated and the educated, if not always of the wealthy, continue none the less, and it is too easily assumed that they generally happen for the same reasons as they did in the old days. Bernard Manning's witty paper to the Cambridge University Congregational Society on 'Some Lapsed Dissenters', which was delivered in 1931 and re-printed in the *Congregational Quarterly* in April 1951, was still able to take substantially that line. The reasons for these changes today are, in fact, very different. For example, people leave Congregationalism for Anglicanism, which takes by far the largest number from us, for at least five reasons other than those of social prestige and those accidental considerations such as the accessibility of a particular church or the character of a particular parson which might, and frequently do, operate in the reverse direction. The first is a theological one. Many people believe that they hear the word of a saving Gospel sounded forth more clearly in the Anglican church than in many Congregational churches. This would have seemed almost incredible to the Dissenters of a couple of generations ago but the influence of popular modernism in the Congregationalism of the last generation makes it seem credible enough today. The second, and even more cogent, reason is devotional. Anglicanism in the modern world has succeeded in providing a more coherent and satisfying form of spiritual discipline than Congregationalism. Its appeal to educated women in particular has been very great in this respect and we have lost many of our best children for this reason. Thirdly, there is a reason which might be called cultural. The good taste exemplified by Anglican liturgical practice and church design, at least since it has overcome its Victorian lapses, has been remarkably resistant to the forces of vulgarization which have been operative over large areas of life, and the re-definition of Anglican teaching about society given by bodies like the Christendom group has had a strong appeal for a limited number of serious-minded Congregationalists of academic background. Fourthly, there is the powerful influence of the Anglican public schools to which many Congregationalists send their children. And, last of all, there is the simple but extremely practical consideration that those who move up into positions of responsibility in modern society have also to move their homes from the provincial town or the suburb to the centre of the city, generally London, and spend many of their week-ends in the country. It is extremely difficult in such a situation to retain effective membership of a Congregational church, whereas the Church of England is comparatively well equipped to minister to those who find themselves so placed.

What is serious for Congregationalism is that it is many of its best children which it loses in this process. They may not be lost to the Church in general, and their contribution may greatly enrich the life of the denomination to which they go, but it is a bad thing for all the churches if too many of them leave the church which produced them. Even if it be accepted that Congregationalism's chief vocation is likely to remain with people of 'the middling sort' it needs a leaven of people whose intellectual and cultural standards are of the highest just as much as it also needs a substantial number of the simple and poor if it is not to become a rigidly one-class church which quickly freezes out from its midst all those who do not conform to the outlook of the majority. We have already seen that the closely knit, democratic character of Congregational church organization, which is in many ways one of the main sources of its strength, does expose it to the danger of always seeking the middle course and the safe and unadventurous. This can only be resisted if some Congregationalists and at least a few particular churches make it their business to seek only the best in theology and ritual and music and architecture and to pioneer in new ways of Christian thought and action without much reference to popular appeal. It is not enough for churches of other denominations to do this and for Congregationalists to learn from their experience. Congregationalism has its own distinctive contribution to make in these matters and, if such efforts are not to degenerate into highbrow preciousness and fail to have any effect on the life of more ordinary churches, it is essential that those who undertake them be in contact and sympathy with the other churches of their own order and that they win a fair measure of their confidence. Otherwise a certain aggressive philistinism, which can already be detected in certain branches of Congregationalism, quickly emerges among those ordinary churches, and any idea or expression or building or hymn-tune which does not readily commend itself to the more self-satisfied type of elderly business man and his wife is in danger of being summarily rejected.

More thought and experiment are obviously required before any way of meeting this need can be confidently prescribed.

There is a case to be made for gathering together some of those Congregationalists with specialized interests in the arts or in politics or in education. Many of these meet at ecumenical gatherings but it might be valuable for them to meet occasionally to look at their vocation in terms of their own tradition, if only in order to define it more precisely in ecumenical gatherings. And there seems to be a very clear need for the establishment of small churches in the central areas of large cities which appeal frankly to those with specialized interests and which should be relieved of the pressure of seeking to justify themselves in terms of the numbers they attract. Congregationalists are rightly suspicious of any proposal which seems to limit church membership only to people of a particular type or interest. But, although this suggestion may involve limiting the appeal of the witness of a particular congregation, its purpose is to broaden the appeal of the denomination as a whole because, as we have seen, its appeal is already unconsciously limited very severely to people of a specific type living in narrowly defined neighbourhoods. The Church must be all things to all men but it is an impossible undertaking for it to try to be that to all of them at the same time. Experience shows that that means only that the lowest common denominator is quickly reached. The foundation of small churches, or of institutions associated with churches, of the Third Programme type, like that initiated by the Church of England at St. Anne's House, Soho, in London, might make a great deal of difference to Congregationalism's ability to retain in the next generation many of its liveliest young people whom it now so frequently loses. Such institutions will fulfil a much more useful function than the proliferation of Congregational societies at universities, which are always in danger of denying to their members the valuable educational influence of the Student Christian Movement.

The most notable experiment along these lines which has so

far been attempted is that undertaken at the Judson Memorial Church in Greenwich Village, New York.[1] The need for such experiments is peculiarly urgent in America, both because of the traditional association of Congregationalism with the highly-educated classes in that land and because of its comparative failure to give them prophetic guidance. But, although its scale is smaller, the need is hardly less real in Britain also, especially in those neighbourhoods where large numbers of educated people who have been brought up in small-town Congregational churches go to live. Central London and, perhaps, the cities of Cardiff and Manchester, would seem to be promising places at which to start such experiments.

It would be false to the main intention of this book if these suggestions were taken to imply that our aim should be to make Congregationalism as self-sufficient and all-embracing a denomination as possible. They are meant to make our distinctive witness more effective and to promote that internal ecumenicity which was spoken of in the first chapter. Some of them might well be promoted on an inter-denominational basis but, if they are, it is of the first importance that they do so in such a way that their influence flows back into the life of the churches and effectively modifies that life. Congregationalists take a prominent part in specialized activities of an inter-denominational kind. The freedom of choice which their ministers enjoy in relation to the work they decide to do makes it very easy for them to do so. But the price they have to pay for this is that their denomination in general is singularly indifferent to their activities in these specialized realms, except when members are gratified by the prestige which such

[1] See *Christianity and Society* (edited by Reinhold Niebuhr in New York, Spring quarter, 1953) for an account of this given by the minister of the Judson Church, Robert W. Spike. The Judson Church is of Baptist origin but has recently made formal links with the Congregational-Christian denomination.

activities occasionally confer. The blame for this state of affairs lies both with those engaged in inter-denominational activities and with the churches. A few enterprises of the kind we have described, organized on a specifically Congregationalist basis, or organized by Congregationalists in association with closely allied denominations like the Baptists or Presbyterians, staffed by people with intimate experience of the ecumenical movement, may serve to make Congregationalism more and not less ecumenical in outlook.

This becomes the more important when it is realized that, broadly speaking, churches of most kinds are becoming increasingly similar to each other. We need to preserve and bring out that which is best in our own heritage but equally firmly we need to set that within a greatly enriched understanding of what the Great Church means and of the fact that our most important possessions as churches are those which all churches have in common, the Scriptures, the preaching, the Sacraments, the fellowship. That is not only ecumenism; we hope that this book has succeeded in showing again that it is also Congregationalism. The implication of this is both that Congregationalists must be prepared to surrender their identity in a wider fellowship of churches, which makes more clearly manifest the true nature of the Church, and that they strive to become more fully and recognizably a part of the universal family of God in their own internal life.

Anyone looking at the actual condition of Congregationalism today must acknowledge that its prospects are extremely uncertain. It may continue to benefit by accessions from other churches, especially in America, but there is not yet much clear sign that its own losses will abate. The forces of revival in theology and church order are active in its midst, but whether they are sufficiently strong to bring about the rapid and painful adjustments necessary for its survival in the modern world as an effective part of the family of God remains to be seen, for the influence of trivialization and 'suburbanization' has gone very deep. Our fathers were men of faith who ventured out into the 'howling wilderness', whether it was that of the North American Continent or that of the England of the Industrial Revolution, and there built churches which were indeed fair gardens of the Lord. We, their children, have to show that we can maintain that inheritance as something more than a series of country clubs. This book has sought to show something of what that might mean. It means a clearer recognition of the true basis of our faith and of the fact that our fight for the freedom of the Spirit has to be fought out anew in our own experience before we can say much to those outside. It also means a reconsideration of our tradition in worship and a determination both to make our church meetings more effective and to find more adequate ways of expressing the communion of the churches with each other. Not least, it means an effort to break out from being a denomination of such limited appeal and to reach toward people of a different type from those who normally associate with us. Congregationalism emphasizes aspects of the Christian faith which are particularly needed in our time. Our best way of commending them to others is by allowing our own life to be judged and reformed by them. The prospect for Congregationalism is good only to the extent to which it partakes of the nature of that one Church to which the divine promise has been given and finds its true life in obedience to its Lord.

Index

Index